Cook Talk with Curtis Grace and Friends

A Collection of Favorite Recipes
From Curtis Grace
And His
Ninth Street House Restaurant

McClanahan Publishing House, Inc.
P.O. Box 100
Kuttawa, Kentucky 42055

Library of Congress Card Number: 88-061583
ISBN 0-913383-10-4

Cover design by: James Asher

Typeset: Gloria Stewart
Illustrations by: Norma Grace
James Asher
Background for front cover by: © Covington Fabric Corp.

Published by McClanahan Publishing House, Inc.
P.O. Box 100
Kuttawa, Kentucky, 42055
Call toll free: 1-800-544-6959

Manufactured in the United States of America

This book is dedicated to my grandchildren:

Haley Megan
Jilanna Leigh
Corey Austin
Rebecca Aubrey
Jayson Danial
Farrah Heather

In memory of...

To Daddy, who always washed the dishes, helped to clean the kitchen, corrected me by saying,"Oh son, I wouldn't do that", teased me about my failure of a molasses mousse—calling it my "molasses moussie".

Curtis Grace, professional caterer, restaurant owner/chef, developed his love and respect for food in early life when he prepared dinners for his working parents. After he married Norma, he was welcomed in their kitchen to help with meals for their growing sons Curtis, Jay, Tim and Bryan.

In the 1970's Curtis and Norma Grace purchased the historic Wallace house, one of the landmarks of Paducah's Lower Town, and opened the popular Ninth Street House restaurant. Their successful catering service, the House of Grace continues to prepare imaginative foods for every occasion.

Cooking classes with James Beard, Julie Dannenbaum and Marion Cunningham have enhanced his culinary skills. Curtis Grace's flair for combining everyday ingredients into exciting dishes and his famous Ninth Street House restaurant have been acknowledged in national magazines and newspapers.

Cook Talk With Curtis Grace and Friends is the second book written by Grace and is an accompaniment to his best seller, **Cooking With Curtis Grace,** published in 1985.

Cook Talk With Curtis Grace and Friends continues to please readers with simple-to-prepare recipes using everyday ingredients. Preparation time is kept to a minimum and many dishes may be prepared ahead of time. The results are irresistible and taste as if hours were spent in the kitchen! From Mushroom Pâté, Cream of Avocado Soup, to Strawberry Aspic, Orange Ginger Pork Chops, Spinach Artichoke Casserole, and Buttermilk Sherbet, **Cook Talk** puts pizzazz in your kitchen routine.

Cook Talk with Curtis Grace and Friends...

One day Miss Jean and I were engaged in conversation when Bruce came in and asked what we were talking about. Jean's reply was, "Bruce, this is none of your business, this is cook talk!"

Table of Contents

Appetizers and Soups

Dining Room, Ninth Street House

Reuben Tarts

1 1/2 8-ounce packages cream cheese
3/4 cup margarine
1 1/2 cups plain flour
1/2 cup mayonnaise
1/4 cup chili sauce
1 16-ounce can sauerkraut, drained
1 8-ounce can corned beef
3/4 cup grated Swiss cheese
paprika

Blend cream cheese, margarine and flour. Chill one hour. Shape in small balls and place in ungreased muffin tins. Press dough on bottom and sides of cups. Mix remaining ingredients for filling. Fill cups and sprinkle with paprika. Bake at 350 degrees until brown.

Makes 18 to 24 tarts

Susan's Mock Oysters

1/4 pound butter
1/2 large onion, chopped
1 large can mushroom pieces, drained
3 stalks celery, chopped
1 green pepper, chopped
1 package frozen chopped broccoli
1 package Kraft Garlic cheese
1 can cream of mushroom soup, undiluted

Melt butter, sauté onion, mushroom pieces, celery and pepper. Cook broccoli as directed, drain well. Blend broccoli and onion mixture. Add cheese and stir until melted. Stir in soup. Serve as a dip or vegetable or spread on finger sandwiches and heat in oven.

Mollie Lea's Franks in Sour Cream

6 frankfurters, cut into 1/2 inch slices
2 tablespoons oil
2 teaspoons sugar
1/4 teaspoon salt
1 tablespoon caraway seed
2 tablespoons flour
1/2 cup water
1 cup sour cream

Brown franks in oil; add sugar, salt and caraway seed. Mix flour with water. Slowly stir into frank mixture. Just before serving add sour cream. Serve from chafing dish with crackers or party rye.

Mollie Lea says her guests mistake it for crabmeat!

Artichoke Frittata

3 6-ounce jars marinated artichoke hearts,
drained and chopped, saving juice
5 medium green onions, chopped
1 clove garlic, minced
8 large eggs, beaten
10 soda crackers, crushed medium
1/2 teaspoon salt
1/8 teaspoon pepper
1 tablespoon minced parsley
dash of Tabasco
1 pound sharp cheese, grated

Special utensils:
9 x 9 inch square glass dish sprayed with non-stick cooking spray when serving as luncheon dish or vegetable; or 9 x 12 glass dish when serving as hors d'oeuvres.

Pour marinade juice from all three jars of artichokes into skillet (it is not all oil, but about 2/3 water). Sauté, using medium heat, the chopped onions and garlic in marinade until soft, which will evaporate part of liquid. Set aside. Chop the drained artichokes into coarse pieces. Set aside. Place eggs in large bowl and beat well. Add crushed crackers, salt, pepper, parsley, Tabasco, onions, garlic and remaining liquid in skillet. Mix until well combined. Add grated cheese and chopped artichoke hearts. Mix until thoroughly blended.

Pour into prepared pan and bake on center rack of preheated 325 degree oven about 40 to 45 minutes or until it puffs up a bit. It will sink when removed from oven. (For 9 x 12 inch dish, bake about 25 to 30 minutes.)

May be served as a luncheon dish, warmed, with green salad. May also be served cold, cut into small squares as hors d'oeuvres.

Miss Jean kept saying she was going to take her camera along on one of our parties to capture our food table. When she did take it and started to take a picture she had brought along her remote control for her television instead of her camera. I told her I was sure Miss Kizzie was home trying to change channels with the camera remote.

Artichoke Appetizers

4 eggs, beaten
2 jars marinated artichoke hearts, chopped and drained
12 crackers, crumbled
9 ounces cheddar cheese, grated
salt, pepper and Tabasco to taste

Mix all ingredients together and bake in an eight inch square glass pan which has been sprayed with a non-stick spray. (Metal pans will turn the artichokes dark.) Bake at 325 degrees 30 to 40 minutes or until firm. To serve, cut into squares.

Artichoke Spread

1 large can artichoke hearts, chopped fine
1 small can green chilies, chopped fine
1/2 cup Parmesan cheese
1/2 cup mayonnaise

Mix all together early in the day and refrigerate to blend flavors. Bake at 350 degrees for 40 minutes in an 8 x 8 inch glass pan which has been coated with cooking spray. Serve with sesame seed crackers.

Garden Gold Cheese Puffs

2 tablespoons butter or margarine
1 small onion, chopped
3 tablespoons flour
1 cup milk
1 teaspoon salt
1/2 teaspoon dry mustard
1/4 teaspoon pepper
1 8-ounce package cream cheese, crumbled
4 eggs, separated
1 cup greens, (turnip or mustard), cooked, chopped, and drained

Melt butter in saucepan over low heat. Add onion and cook slowly for 5 minutes. Stir in flour, then the milk. Add salt, dry mustard and pepper. Cook and stir until very thick. Cool slightly. Mix in cream cheese, egg yolks, and greens. Beat egg whites until stiff but not dry. Fold into greens mixture. Pour into an ungreased 2 quart casserole. Bake at 325 degrees for approximately 1 hour or until knife inserted into the center comes out clean.

Serves 6

Calcuttas

12 large prunes
Port wine
Major Grey's Chutney
sliced bacon

Soak prunes overnight in Port wine. Drain and dry, then remove pits. Fill prunes with chutney. Wrap with bacon and broil until crisp. Stick with pick and serve warm.

Ruth's Clam Rolls

sandwich bread
melted butter
2 tablespoons minced onion
2 tablespoons butter
dash Worcestershire sauce
salt
pepper
dash garlic salt
1 tablespoon flour
1 7-ounce can minced clams, undrained

Trim crust from sandwich bread. Roll very thin with rolling pin. Spread with melted butter and set aside.

Cook minced onion in butter. Add Worcestershire sauce, salt and pepper to taste, and garlic salt. Stir in flour, and add clams. Bring mixture to boil and cook for 1 minute. Spread on slices of bread and roll. Refrigerate until ready to use. Cut in half and brush with melted butter. Bake at 400 degrees about 10 minutes until light brown. Serve hot.

At a cocktail party Dr. Sam French said,
'If any of these are left over, send them to heaven'.

Mrs. Dobson's Chopped Liver Pâté

1 pound livers (chicken or calf)
2 onions, minced
chicken fat
3 or 4 hard boiled eggs
salt
pepper
garlic salt, optional

Boil, broil or sauté liver according to personal preference. Sauté onions in chicken fat until lightly browned. Mix liver, onions and eggs together or put through a meat grinder. Add enough fat to hold mixture together and mix well. Add seasonings to taste. Chill before serving.

Crabmeat Ring Mold

1 cup tomato soup
1 envelope unflavored gelatin
1 small package cream cheese
1 cup mayonnaise
1/3 cup chopped celery
1/3 cup chopped onions
1/3 cup chopped cucumbers
2 pounds crabmeat

Heat tomato soup. Prepare unflavored gelatin as directed on package. Add to tomato soup. Add cream cheese and mix well. Add remaining ingredients and pour into greased ring mold. Refrigerate until time to serve.

Mushroom Pâté

1 pound chicken livers
1 pound fresh mushrooms, washed and sliced
3/4 pound butter, softened
1/2 cup green onions, chopped
1/2 teaspoon thyme
1/2 teaspoon salt
1/8 teaspoon nutmeg
1/2 cup cognac
parsley sprigs for garnish

In a large skillet, sauté chicken livers and mushrooms in 1/4 pound of the butter until livers are no longer pink. With slotted spoon, remove livers and mushrooms to a blender or food processor. Reduce liquid in skillet, then add to liver-mushroom mixture along with onions and remaining butter. Blend and add seasonings, then the cognac. Adjust seasonings, adding more cognac if desired. Blend until smooth and pour into a 3-cup mold that has been lightly oiled. Cover and chill until firm. Unmold, garnish with parsley, and serve with plain crackers or melba rounds.

Serves 12 to 14

Snow Pea Pods Stuffed with Sesame Pork

8 ounces cooked pork, diced small
1 scallion, finely chopped
1/4 cup fresh bean sprouts, blanched and finely chopped
1 tablespoon diced sweet red pepper
1/2 cup fresh diced water chestnuts
1 tablespoon soy sauce
1 tablespoon oyster sauce
a few dashes of sesame oil
20 fresh pea pods, cleaned, with threads removed

Toss together pork, scallion, bean sprouts, red pepper, water chestnuts, soy sauce, oyster sauce and sesame oil. Place pea pods in boiling salted water for approximately 45 seconds, remove immediately and plunge into ice cold water to stop the cooking process. With a sharp paring knife, split open the pods on the straight side, so that they resemble little canoes. Fill pods generously with pork mixture.

Chutney Frosted Cheese Spread

4 cups cheddar cheese, grated
2 cloves garlic, crushed
2 3-ounce packages cream cheese, room temperature
2 teaspoons curry powder
3/4 cup chopped green onions
4 tablespoons mayonnaise
salt to taste
1 9-ounce jar Major Grey's Chutney, chopped
1/4 cup green onions, chopped

Mix cheddar cheese, garlic, cream cheese, curry powder, chopped green onions and mayonnaise until well blended. Season to taste.

Spread cheese mixture into 7-inch quiche pan with removable bottom. Refrigerate overnight. Frost top of cheese with chutney. Sprinkle ring of green onions around outer edge. Remove sides. Serve with crackers or bread.

Serves 16

*May be refrigerated for one week or frozen. If frozen, defrost overnight in refrigerator.

This spread has the velvety softness of a blend of cheeses, enhanced by the flavors of curry and chutney. Use a fluted quiche pan to mold the cheese with a pretty ruffled edge.

Crab Pâté

1 can cream of mushroom soup
1 envelope unflavored gelatin
3 tablespoons cold water
3/4 cup mayonnaise
8 ounces cream cheese, room temperature
1 6 1/2-ounce can crabmeat*
2 tablespoons grated onion
1 cup chopped celery
2 tablespoons chopped parsley
1 teaspoon dill weed

Heat soup; dissolve gelatin in cold water and add to soup. Stir until well dissolved. Add remaining ingredients, stirring well to blend. Place into mold that has been coated with mayonnaise. Refrigerate until firm. Unmold on bed of greens. Serve with crackers.

*shrimp may be used

Carla's Shrimp Dip Mold

3/4 cup boiling water
1 small package lemon gelatin
1 tablespoon lemon juice
3 tablespoons horseradish
1 package unflavored gelatin, dissolved in 1/4 cup cold water
1 12-ounce bottle chili sauce
2 4-ounce cans shrimp, drained

Dissolve lemon gelatin in boiling water, cool slightly; add remaining ingredients and pour into well oiled 3 1/2 cup mold. Chill until set. Serve with club crackers.

People ask if I have ever been late for a party and my reply is "No, but I have been a month early."

Our caravan of people, food, dishes, etc. pulled into the driveway to find the host and hostess working in their lawn. They were as surprised as we were to discover we were a month early. I had to have someone drive me home. – I was too weak!

Baked Pâté Cedaredge

1 1/2 pounds chicken livers
1/2 pound veal stew meat
1 medium onion, chopped
1 clove garlic, minced
4 tablespoons butter
2 eggs
1/4 cup all-purpose flour
1/2 teaspoon ginger
1/2 teaspoon allspice
salt and pepper to taste
1 cup heavy cream

Sauté chicken livers, veal, onions, and garlic in butter. Place in food processor with remaining ingredients and process until smooth. Pour into buttered and floured 1 1/2 quart baking pan. Cover tightly and bake in 325 degree oven 1 1/2 to 2 hours. Chill and unmold onto platter. Serve with crackers.

Serves 6 to 8

Succotash Soup

1/2 stick of butter
1 medium size onion, chopped
1/2 teaspoon curry powder
salt and pepper to taste
1 8 3/4 ounce can cream style corn
2 10 1/2 ounce cans oyster stew
1 16 ounce can Italian tomatoes
8 ounces sour cream

Melt butter, add chopped onion, cook over low heat until transparent, add curry powder, salt and pepper, heat and mix well. Chop and add all the other ingredients. Mix well and heat. This is better if made the day before serving. Serve hot or cold.

6 to 8 cups

Cheesy Chicken Chowder

1 cup carrot, shredded
1/4 cup onion, chopped
4 tablespoons butter
1/4 cup flour
2 cups milk
1 13 1/4-ounce can chicken broth
1 cup cooked chicken, diced
2 tablespoons dry white wine
1/2 teaspoon celery seed
1/2 teaspoon Worcestershire sauce
1 cup sharp cheese, shredded

In a heavy saucepan, sauté carrot and onion in butter until tender but not brown. Blend in flour, milk and broth. Stir constantly until thickened and bubbly.

Stir in chicken, wine, celery seed and Worcestershire sauce. Add the grated cheese and stir until thickened. Season to taste.

Serves 4 or 5

Cream of Avocado Soup

2 large avocados
1/2 teaspoon salt
1 cup half and half
2 teaspoons lemon juice
2 cups rich chicken broth
1/4 cup dry sherry
lime or sour cream

Cut the avocados in half. Remove the seeds and scoop out the flesh. Place the avocado flesh, salt, half and half, and lemon juice in a blender or food processor. Blend to a smooth puree. Pour puree into a pan or bowl. Heat chicken broth to boiling. Slowly add hot broth to puree. Add sherry. May be served hot or cold.

If serving hot, heat but do not boil! If serving cold, refrigerate for several hours and serve in cold cups or bowls. Garnish with a thin slice of lime or a dollop of sour cream.

Serves 6 to 8 as a first course

Linda's Asparagus Leek Chowder

3 cups sliced fresh mushrooms
3 large leeks, sliced diagonally in 3/4 inch length, use 1/2 way up leek
1 10-ounce package frozen asparagus
6 tablespoons butter
1/2 teaspoon salt
dash pepper
3 tablespoons flour
2 cups rich chicken stock
2 cups half and half cream
1 12-ounce can white corn or hominy
1 tablespoon chopped pimento

In a large saucepan cook mushrooms, leeks and asparagus in butter until tender, but not browned, or for about 10 minutes. Stir in salt, pepper and flour. Add chicken broth and half and half. Cook until thick and creamy, stirring constantly. Do not let boil. Add corn or hominy and pimento. Correct seasonings.

Serves 6 to 8 persons

Cold Watercress Soup

2 bunches watercress, leaves only
2 small zucchini, sliced
2 leeks
1 large potato, peeled and sliced
1 small head butter lettuce
2 scallions
1/2 cup parsley leaves
1 tablespoon chicken bouillon granules
2 cups water
1 cup whipping cream
sour cream or sherry, optional

Slice all vegetables. Simmer in bouillon granules and water until tender, 20 to 30 minutes. Purée in food processor and return to pot. Add whipping cream and season to taste. Chill.

If desired, place dollop of sour cream or a tablespoon of sherry in each soup bowl.

Serves 6 to 8 as a first course

Bunny's Pumpkin Soup

2 tablespoons butter
2 ribs celery, chopped
2 onions, chopped
2 cups cooked pumpkin, mashed
4 cups chicken or beef stock,
  or combination of both
1 bay leaf
1 teaspoon dried basil
1 teaspoon dried thyme
1 cup heavy cream
sour cream

Melt butter in large saucepan. Sauté celery and onions in butter until transparent. Add pumpkin, stock and spices. Simmer over low heat 30 minutes to one hour, stirring often. Just before serving, stir in cream and reheat. Do not let boil. Soup can be served without adding cream. Add dollop of sour cream to each bowl.

Freezes well with or without cream.

An original recipe from my friend Bunny,
who has many originals.

Okra and Tomato Gumbo

1/4 cup vegetable oil
1/2 cup green pepper, chopped
1/4 cup onion, chopped
1/4 cup celery, chopped
1/4 cup plain flour
4 cups chicken stock
3/4 pound okra, cut in 1 inch pieces
1/8 teaspoon cayenne pepper
6 drops Tabasco
1/2 teaspoon thyme
6 tomatoes, peeled and diced
2 cups cooked rice
1 tablespoon cilantro leaves

Sauté green pepper, onion and celery in oil. Slowly stir in flour. Add chicken stock gradually, stirring constantly. Add remaining ingredients except rice and coriander leaves. Simmer until vegetables are tender. Add rice and cilantro leaves.

Serves 8 to 10

Spiked Lobster Soup

1 can cream of mushroom soup
1 can chicken soup with rice
1 large can evaporated milk
2 ounces lobster or crabmeat, fresh or frozen
1/4 cup bourbon or sherry

Stir together soups and milk. Add lobster or crabmeat. At the last minute, stir in bourbon or sherry.

This soup can be made ahead of time, but the liquor must be added at the last minute.

This can be used as a first course.

Apple Carrot Soup

6 tablespoons butter
2 cups diced green pippin apples, unpeeled
1 cup diced celery
1 cup diced onion
2 cups scraped, diced carrots
8 cups rich chicken broth
1 cup half and half
salt
white pepper

Melt butter in heavy 4-quart pot. Add apple, celery, onion and carrots. Sauté over very low heat for 30 minutes, stirring every 5 minutes. (Mixture is cooked uncovered and should not brown.) Add chicken broth, stir and simmer uncovered for 1 hour.

Place sieve over a clean pot and pour soup through sieve. Put vegetables in sieve into food processor with steel knife (or blender or food mill) and process until completely smooth. Add puréed vegetables to stock in pot and bring to a simmer. Add cream, salt and pepper to taste and heat just 2 minutes.

Serves 12

Breads, Brunch and Beverages

The Ninth Street House

Maui Mango Bread

3/4 cup butter
1 1/4 cups sugar
3 eggs
1 teaspoon vanilla
1/4 teaspoon coconut extract
2 cups flour
1/2 teaspoon salt
2 teaspoons soda
1 teaspoon cinnamon
1/2 cup walnuts, chopped
2 cups mango fruit, diced with pulp
(2 to 3 large mangoes)

Cream butter and sugar. Add eggs one at a time. With third egg add vanilla and coconut extract. Add 1 cup of the flour, salt, soda and cinnamon. Stir with spatula. Add remaining flour, nuts and mango. Mix well. Pour into greased and floured pan. Bake at 350 degrees for 50 to 60 minutes.

This was served to us for breakfast at Cedarberry B & B along with fresh grilled trout, fried potatoes, fresh fruits and melons, topped off with lots of warm friendship.

Note: Buy mangoes when they are overripe and price reduced. Prepare and freeze in 2 cup measures for each recipe.

Rhubarb Bread

2 1/2 cups all-purpose flour
1 teaspoon soda
3/4 teaspoon salt
3/4 cup butter
1 1/2 cups brown sugar, packed
1 egg
1 teaspoon lemon extract
2 teaspoons lemon rind, grated
1 cup buttermilk
1 1/2 cups fresh rhubarb, finely diced
3/4 to 1 cup pecans, chopped
1 tablespoon butter, melted
1/2 cup sugar

Sift flour, soda and salt; set aside. Cream butter and add brown sugar gradually, beating until light and fluffy. Add egg and beat well. Stir in extract and rind. Add dry ingredients alternately with buttermilk, mixing well after each addition. Stir in rhubarb and nuts. Pour batter into lightly greased bundt pan or two 8 x 4 x 2 inch loaf pans. Combine butter and sugar and sprinkle over top of batter. Bake at 350 degrees for 1 hour and 10 minutes (less for smaller loaf pans). Freezes well.

Southern Spoon Bread

1 cup cornmeal
3 cups sweet milk
1 teaspoon salt
1 teaspoon baking powder
2 tablepsoons salad oil or melted shortening
3 well beaten egg yolks
3 stiffly beaten egg whites

Cook cornmeal and 2 cups milk until the consistency of mush. Remove from heat; add salt, baking powder, salad oil and 1 cup milk. Stir in egg yolks, fold in egg whites. Bake in greased 2- quart baking dish at 325 degrees for 1 hour or until mixture doesn't adhere to knife. Serve immediately.

Serves 6

Fast Italian Bread

1 package dry yeast
3/4 cup plus 2 tablespoons warm water
(105 - 115 degrees F)
2 1/2 cups unbleached all-purpose flour
1 1/2 teaspoons sugar
1 1/2 teaspoons salt
2 tablespoons cornmeal

In a 2-cup liquid measure, stir yeast into 1/4 cup warm water and let stand for 10 minutes. Use the metal blade of a food processor to process the flour, sugar, and salt for 20 seconds. Add remaining warm water to the yeast. With the motor running, pour yeast mixture through the feed tube in a steady stream as fast as the flour mixture absorbs it. Process until the dough is smooth and elastic and just cleans the side of the bowl. (If the dough is too moist to clean the side of the bowl, add flour by tablespoons through the feed tube. If it is too dry, add warm water by teaspoons.) Process about 30 to 40 seconds more to knead the dough.

Sprinkle a baking sheet with the cornmeal. With lightly floured hands, remove the dough from the work bowl, shape into 16-inch loaf and place on baking sheet. Cover it with oiled plastic wrap and let rise until doubled in bulk, about 45 minutes. Preheat the oven to 375 degrees. Slash top of the loaf and lightly spray the dough with water. Bake about 20 minutes until brown and sounds hollow when tapped with a wooden spoon.

Connie McClain's Corn Light Bread

4 cups self-rising cornmeal
1 cup plain flour
1 1/2 cups sugar
2 teaspoons salt
1 teaspoon baking soda
1/2 cup vegetable oil
4 cups sour milk or buttermilk*

Mix all dry ingredients together in a large bowl. Add liquid ingredients and stir until blended well. Spray 2 loaf pans with vegetable spray and divide batter into each. Bake at 365 degrees until breaks away from side of pan. Remove from pans while hot and immediately wrap loosely in wax paper. This will steam loaves. When cool, wrap tightly.

*in a 4 cup measure place 2/3 cup vinegar and add sweet milk to the top of measure and stir. This works better than sour milk or buttermilk.

Makes 2 loaves

Freezes well and can be cooked in an angel food cake pan.

Freeze Biscuits

1/4 cup shortening
2 cups sifted self-rising flour
2/3 cup cold milk

Cut shortening into flour until particles are like coarse meal. Stir in milk to make a soft dough. Turn dough out on lightly floured board or cloth and knead until smooth. Roll dough out and cut with floured cutter. Place on ungreased baking sheet, brush tops lightly with milk and put in freezer.

When frozen hard, about 1 hour, remove and put in a plastic bag. When ready to use, remove from freezer and place on ungreased baking sheet. Bake in preheated 450 degree oven for 12 to 15 minutes.

Note: Do not let biscuits thaw before baking, and be sure oven temperature has reached 450 degrees.

Hushpuppies

2 cups meal
1/2 cup flour
1 teaspoon baking powder
1/2 teaspoon salt
1/2 teaspoon soda
buttermilk (for stiff dough)
1/2 cup onions, chopped
2 eggs, beaten

Combine dry ingredients. Add enough buttermilk to make a stiff dough. Add onions and eggs, mixing thoroughly. Form into balls and fry in a deep fat fryer until brown.

This recipe
was used in the dining room at
Kentucky Dam Village where I worked while in high school.

Danish Puff

1 cup flour
1/2 cup butter
1 tablespoon water
1 cup water
1/2 cup butter
1 cup flour
3 eggs
1/2 teaspoon almond extract
1 cup powdered sugar
1 tablespoon butter
1/2 teaspoon almond extract
cream
chopped nuts

Mix flour, butter and 1 tablespoon water as for pie crust and pat onto cookie sheet in two long, 3 inch wide strips. Heat water and butter to boiling point. Remove from heat and add flour immediately. Stir until smooth. Add eggs, one at a time, beating well after each addition. Add extract; spread on strips. Bake at 350 degrees for 55 to 60 minutes. Cool.

For icing, combine powdered sugar, butter and almond extract. Add cream to spread easily and sprinkle chopped nuts on top.

Creole Eggs Curtis Lee

1 medium size onion, chopped fine*
2 tablespoons bacon fat
1 15-ounce can tomatoes
dash Tabasco sauce
salt and pepper to taste
1/2 cup butter
3 tablespoons flour, heaping
1 cup milk
8 large hard boiled eggs
1 cup toasted crumbs

Sauté onions in bacon fat. Add tomatoes and simmer until onions are well done. Add Tabasco, salt and pepper to taste. This mixture should be highly seasoned. Make a white sauce of 1/2 the butter, all the flour and milk. Sauce should be thick. Add tomato mixture to white sauce and stir well. Slice eggs into well buttered casserole, pour tomato mixture over eggs. Mix bread crumbs with remaining butter, and sprinkle on top. Bake at 325 degrees until crumbs are brown.

Serves 6 to 8

*chopped bell peppers may be added with onions

Mushroom Sausage Strudel

2 pounds bulk pork sausage
2 pounds fresh mushrooms, minced and thoroughly dried
1/4 cup minced shallots or green onions
6 tablespoons butter
2 tablespoons vegetable oil
salt and pepper
16 ounces cream cheese
8 sheets phyllo pastry
3/4 cup melted butter
1 cup seasoned bread crumbs

Sauté sausage until no longer pink, crumbling into small pieces. Drain and set aside. Sauté mushrooms, shallots or green onions in butter and oil over moderate heat, stirring frequently. Cook until pieces separate and liquid has evaporated. Add salt and pepper and combine mushroom mixture with sausage and cream cheese, blending well.

Place one sheet pastry on lightly dampened towel. Quickly brush with melted butter and sprinkle with a few bread crumbs. Top with second sheet and repeat procedure. Repeat with third sheet. Top with fourth sheet and butter, but omit crumbs. Spoon half the sausage-mushroom mixture along narrow edge of phyllo pastry, leaving a two-inch border along sides. Fold in sides and roll up *pastry. Repeat procedure. Bake on buttered baking sheet at 400 degrees for 20 minutes or until golden brown. Cut into serving size pieces.*

Serves 8 to 10

Delicious with fruits and melons for brunch

Daus Brown Haus All in One Quiche

1 1/2 cups milk
1/2 cup biscuit mix
6 tablespoons butter, room temperature
3 eggs
pinch of salt
1 cup diced ham, turkey, shrimp, chicken, bacon or vegetables
2 green onions, chopped
1 4-ounce can sliced mushrooms, drained
1 cup grated sharp cheddar cheese

Preheat oven to 350 degrees. Combine milk, biscuit mix, butter, eggs and salt in blender and mix well. Turn into ungreased deep dish 9-inch pie plate. Add meat, shellfish or vegetables, poking into batter. Top with onions, mushrooms, and cheese. Bake until top is golden, about 45 minutes. Let stand 10 minutes before serving.

Serves 6

Frances Williams' Scalloped Rhubarb

3 cups stale bread, cubed
1 stick butter, melted
2 cups uncooked rhubarb, diced (I use frozen)
1 cup sugar
4 teaspoons water

Combine all ingredients, mixing well. Place in a buttered oblong pan. Put one teaspoon water in each corner of pan. Bake at 325 degrees for 45 minutes.

Serves 6

Glazed Bacon

1/2 pound sliced lean bacon
(If possible, buy slab bacon and have it sliced)
1/2 cup light brown sugar, packed
1 tablespoon Dijon mustard
2 tablespoons red or white wine

Place bacon in large pan and bake in a preheated 350 degree oven for ten minutes. Drain off all fat. At this point bacon should be almost crisp. Combine sugar, mustard and wine until smooth. Pour half this mixture over bacon and return to oven for ten more minutes. Turn bacon, cover with remaining glaze, continue to bake until golden brown. Remove and place on waxed paper. Serve warm or cool.

Delicious!

Compliments of Cedarberry Bed and Breakfast

Cheese Soufflé

1 level tablespoon butter
1 level tablespoon flour
1 cup grated cheese
1 cup milk
salt
pepper
3 eggs, separated

Put butter and flour together in pan; stir on low heat until blended without browning. Then add the grated cheese, milk, salt and pepper. Set aside to cool. (This step cannot be omitted.) Beat whites and yolks separately, then add mixture in sauce pan to beaten egg yolks and blend thoroughly. Lastly fold in whites stiffly beaten; turn the soufflé into a well-greased pan or dish. Bake in a moderate oven about 25 minutes.
Serve immediately or it may fall.

Do not think because you have made soufflés before you can improve on this--go implicitly by this recipe and it will be absolutely perfect.

Miss Mama's Hot Spiced Percolator Punch

9 cups unsweetened pineapple juice
9 cups cranberry juice
4 1/2 cups water
1 cup brown sugar
4 1/2 teaspoons whole cloves
4 sticks cinnamon
1/4 teaspoon salt

Place juices and water in the bottom of a 30-cup percolator. In the top basket place sugar, spices and salt. Plug in and perk! Very good!

Serves 36 (1/2 cup servings)

Jo's Banana Punch

6 bananas, mashed
1 6-ounce can frozen orange juice concentrate
1 6-ounce can frozen lemonade concentrate
4 cups sugar
7 cups water
a few drops of yellow food coloring
ginger ale, chilled

Mix and freeze all ingredients except ginger ale. Remove from freezer 2 hours before serving time. Length of time can depend on temperature. Place in punch bowl and add ginger ale to fill bowl just before serving. Should be very slushy. Very good served in extremely hot weather. It is sweet and you may wish to adjust sugar to your taste.

Serves 32

Ninth Street Stack

small ice cubes
1 1/2 to 2 ounces blended whiskey
sweet and sour mix
1 slice each orange, lime and stemmed cherries

Place ice in high ball glass and add blended whiskey. Top off with homemade sweet and sour mix and garnish with fruit.

For homemade sweet and sour mix:
Combine 2 ounces freshly squeezed orange juice, with pulp and seeds, and add 1 ounce Roses lime juice.

Note: Fresh juices make this cocktail more aromatic. Only use bourbon on request. Blended whiskey is softer and blends better.

Salads, Salad Dressings, and Sauces

Vaughan - Blythe House

Cold Beef Salad with Spinach Dressing

julienne strips of leftover roast beef
celery, sliced
green onions, both white and green parts, sliced
salt and pepper, to taste

Dressing:
mayonnaise
fresh spinach leaves

Toss beef, celery, and onions together. Place individual servings loosely on lettuce leaves. Place mayonnaise in blender and add fresh spinach leaves until desired color is obtained. Spoon dressing over cold beef and garnish with tomato wedges.

A delicious way of using leftover roast beef! Amounts are not specified because you simply use what you have on hand.

Dottie's Spinach Salad

Salad:
1 10-ounce package fresh spinach, washed, drained and torn
1 12-ounce carton cottage cheese, rinsed
1/2 cup pecans, chopped

Dressing:
1/2 cup sour cream
1/4 cup sugar
2 tablespoons vinegar
2 tablespoons horseradish
1/2 teaspoon dry mustard
1/4 teaspoon salt

Combine spinach, cottage cheese and pecans into large serving bowl. Mix together ingredients for dressing, then combine with spinach mixture.

Serves 4

Joyce's Spinach Rice Salad

1 1/3 cups water
2/3 cup long grain rice
1 teaspoon lemon juice
1/2 teaspoon salt
1/2 bay leaf
1/2 cup Italian dressing
2 cups fresh spinach leaves, chopped
1/3 cup diced pepper
1/3 cup frozen peas, defrosted
2 tablespoons parsley, snipped
2 green onions, finely chopped
1 2-ounce jar pimento, chopped
1 medium tomato, seeded and cubed
4 slices bacon, cooked, drained, and crumbled

Bring water to a boil. Add rice, lemon juice, salt and bay leaf. Cover and reduce heat to warm. Steam rice until all moisture is absorbed. Remove bay leaf and toss with 1/4 dressing. Refrigerate until chilled.

Add remaining salad dressing and ingredients except bacon. Correct seasonings, then cover and chill. At serving time, mix in crumbled bacon and serve in clear glass bowl.

Serves 6 to 8

Good hot weather salad!
This was served to us on a picnic in Aspen, Colorado.

Avocado Surprise

2 large ripe avocados
lemon juice, fresh or bottled
lettuce leaves

Filling:
2 cups cooked chicken, diced
1 cup orange sections
1/2 cup green grapes, cut in half
1/4 cup walnuts or pecans, chopped
1/4 cup onion, finely chopped

Dressing:
5 tablespoons olive oil
2 tablespoons lemon juice
2 tablespoons parsley, chopped
1 teaspoon dried basil
salt and pepper

At serving time, cut avocados in half lengthwise. Peel and brush with lemon juice. Combine filling ingredients and chill for 1 hour. Mix dressing ingredients in jar. Mix filling and dressing (shake dressing well first) and heap on avocado halves. Arrange on bed of lettuce leaves.

Note: For elegant, alfresco summer lunches the avocado is a savory kitchen quicky. Crown the nutty fruit with a scoop of chicken salad. Serve with warm rolls and chilled Chablis.

Curried Chicken Salad Rounds

3/4 cup cooked chicken, cubed
1/2 cup celery, chopped
1 tablespoon minced onion
1 tablespoon lemon juice
1/2 teaspoon curry
1/3 cup mayonnaise
6 slices bread
butter or margarine
pineapple slices
1 8-ounce package cream cheese
2 or 3 tablespoons syrup from pineapple
1/4 cup chopped nuts

Combine chicken, celery, onion, lemon juice, curry, and mayonnaise for salad. Cut bread in rounds the same size as pineapple. Butter bread. Spread chicken salad on 6 slices. Place on pineapple rings. Mix cream cheese and pineapple syrup to make icing. Decorate with pineapple and nuts.

Serves 6

Ozie's Congealed Chicken Curry Asparagus

12 to 16 asparagus spears
1 small box lemon gelatin
sliced stuffed olives
1 2/3 cups chicken stock
2 packages unflavored gelatin
1 can cream of chicken soup
1 cup mayonnaise
2 teaspoons curry powder
1 tablespoon Worcestershire sauce
2 1/2 cups cooked chicken
1 cup chopped celery
1/2 cup almonds

Drain liquid from asparagus and add enough water to make 1 1/2 cups. Beat and add to lemon gelatin. Arrange asparagus spears and olives in 2 quart mold. Pour in 1/2 of gelatin mixture. Let jell. Pour in remaining mixture. Combine chicken stock, unflavored gelatin, chicken soup, mayonnaise, curry powder and Worcestershire sauce and cook for 5 minutes. Add cooked chicken, celery and almonds. Chill and pour over gelatin mixture.

Carolyn's Chicken Salad

1 small cantaloupe, quartered, seeds removed
1 cup cooked chicken, cubed
1/2 cup seedless grapes, halved
1/4 cup slivered almonds, toasted
1/2 cup celery, chopped
1/2 cup sour cream
1/4 cup mayonnaise
1 teaspoon soy sauce
1/4 teaspoon salt
1/2 teaspoon curry powder
1/2 tablespoon candied ginger, finely chopped
parsley for garnish

Carefully remove pulp of cantaloupe and cut the fruit into cubes. Combine cantaloupe, chicken, grapes, almonds and celery. Fold together sour cream, mayonnaise, soy sauce, salt, curry and ginger. Carefully add to chicken and grape mixture, then spoon into cantaloupe shells. Garnish with parsley.

Serves 4

Chicken Apricot Salad

1/4 cup mayonnaise
1/4 cup sour cream
1 cup yogurt
1/3 cup milk
2 tablespoons lemon juice
2 teaspoons Dijon mustard
1 teaspoon salt
1 cup dried apricots, diced
3 cups cooked chicken, diced
1 cup celery, chopped
1/3 cup finely chopped scallions
crisp lettuce leaves

Blend mayonnaise, sour cream, yogurt, milk, lemon juice, mustard and salt in large bowl. Add apricots, chicken, celery and scallions. Toss lightly, combining well. Chill. Serve on lettuce leaves. Sprinkle with additional chopped apricots if desired.

Shoe Peg Corn Salad

1 cup sugar
3/4 cup vinegar
1 tablespoon water
1/2 cup salad oil
1 teaspoon black pepper
1 green pepper, chopped
1/2 cup celery, chopped
1 cup chopped onion
1 can shoe peg or white corn, drained
1 can small green peas, drained
1 can French style green beans, drained
1 2-ounce jar pimentos

Bring sugar, vinegar, water, oil and black pepper to a boil for the dressing. Set aside. Mix green pepper, celery, onion, corn, peas, green beans and pimentos together and pour dressing over these. Stir once to mix. Cover and refrigerate overnight. Drain before serving.

Serves 12

Jo's Jellied Potato Salad

5 cups diced cooked potatoes
1 tablespoon vinegar
2 teaspoons salt
1 cup chopped onion
1 teaspoon celery seed
1 1/2 cups mayonnaise or salad dressing
2 small packages lemon gelatin
2 1/2 cups boiling water
1/4 cup vinegar
1/4 cup cold water
9 green pepper rings
9 red pepper rings or pimento strips
1 cup diced cucumbers

Sprinkle potatoes with vinegar and salt. Toss with onion, celery seed, and salad dressing; chill. Meanwhile, dissolve gelatin in boiling water. Add vinegar. Reserve 1 1/3 cups of this mixture. Add cold water to remaining mixture. Pour into 9 x 9 x 2 inch pan. Chill until slightly thick. Arrange green and red pepper rings in gelatin. Chill until set. Chill remaining gelatin until partially set, then beat until soft peaks form. Fold in potato salad and cucumbers. Spoon over gelatin in pan, chill until set. Invert to unmold and cut into squares.

Serves 9

Cooked Pimento Cheese

1 small can pimento, chopped
1 pound Velveeta cheese
1 tablespoon flour
5 tablespoons sugar
1 egg
1 tablespoon mayonnaise
1/4 cup vinegar

Place all ingredients in top of double boiler and cook until smooth. (Use an electric mixer if necessary.) Refrigerate.

My mother obtained this recipe while working at an ordinance plant in Viola, Kentucky during World War II. Good, inexpensive, and keeps well.

Cucumber Cream Salad

1 small package lime gelatin
1 cup hot water
1 teaspoon salt
2 tablespoons vinegar
1 teaspoon onion juice
1/2 cup mayonnaise
1 cup sour cream
2 cups cucumber, finely chopped and drained

Dissolve gelatin in hot water. Chill until slightly thickened. Add remaining ingredients, combining well. Pour into mold that has been lightly coated with mayonnaise. Refrigerate until firm. Unmold on bed of greens and garnish with cherry tomatoes.

Frances Williams' Garden Salad

1 tomato soup can filled with water
1/2 cup vinegar
1 cup sugar
2 small boxes raspberry jello
1 package unflavored gelatin, dissolved as directed
2 cans tomato soup
1 green pepper, chopped
2 cups grated cabbage
1 chopped onion
1 cup chopped celery
dash black pepper
salt to taste

Topping:
4 ounces cream cheese
2 tablespoons salad dressing

Bring water, vinegar and sugar to a boil. Add jello and gelatin and let cool. Add tomato soup, then mix with vegetables and seasonings. Refrigerate overnight.

Prepare topping by mixing cream cheese with salad dressing. Spread over salad.

Serves 12

Red Russian Salad

2 envelopes unflavored gelatin
1 cup cold tomato juice
2 cups tomato juice, heated to boiling
1/2 cup red Russian dressing
1 cup finely chopped green pepper
1/2 cup finely chopped celery

In a large bowl, sprinkle unflavored gelatin over cold juice; let stand 1 minute. Add hot juice and stir until gelatin is completely dissolved; stir in red Russian dressing. Chill, stirring occasionally, until mixture is consistency of unbeaten egg whites. Fold in green pepper and celery. Turn into an 11 x 7 inch baking pan or 5 cup mold or bowl and chill until firm.

Serves 6

Mustard Ring

8 eggs, beaten
1 1/2 cups sugar
2 tablespoons dry mustard
1 cup cider vinegar
1 cup water
1 teaspoon salt
2 packages unflavored gelatin
1/2 cup cold water
1 pint cream, whipped

Mix first six ingredients together in heavy sauce pan. Cook over medium heat, stirring constantly, until custard-like consistency. Dissolve gelatin in water. Stir mixture of gelatin and water into hot custard until dissolved. Remove from heat and cool. When completely cooled fold in whipped cream. Place mixture in mold that has been coated with mayonnaise. When firm, unmold on tray with bed of greens. Garnish with grapes.

Very good with pork!

Serves 8

Swedish Salad

3 hard boiled egg yolks
1 cup whipping cream
5 tablespoons sugar
5 tablespoons white vinegar
bibb lettuce or leaf lettuce
3 or 4 green onions
3 hard boiled egg whites
saltine crackers

Crumble egg yolks and mix with cream, sugar and vinegar. Wash and tear greens. Chill. Chopped onions may be added or omitted. Chop egg whites and add to the greens and onions. When ready to serve, shake dressing well and pour over greens. Serve with saltine crackers.

Cranberry Fluff

2 cups raw cranberries, ground
3 cups miniature marshmallows
3/4 cup granulated sugar
2 cups tart apples, diced and unpared
1/2 cup grapes, cut in half with seeds removed
1/2 cup toasted pecans, chopped
pinch salt
1 cup heavy cream, whipped

Combine cranberries, marshmallows and sugar. Let set overnight. Add apples, grapes, pecans, and salt. Fold together gently with whipped cream. Chill. Turn into serving bowl, or spoon into individual lettuce cups. Trim with a cluster of grapes, if desired.

Serves 8 to 10

Wonderful for the holidays!

"When my son Jay was in grade school, he told me one of his teachers, Mrs. Mathis, would like my recipe for 'Cranberry Flop'!"

Spicy Peach Cranberry Ring

1 16-ounce can peach halves
water
1 teaspoon whole cloves
3 inch stick cinnamon
1/4 cup vinegar
1 small package lemon gelatin
1 package frozen cranberry-orange relish
    or:
        1 cup fresh cranberries
        1/2 unpeeled orange
        1/3 cup granulated sugar
1 3/4 cups hot water
1 small package cherry gelatin

Drain peaches and set aside; add water to syrup to make 1 3/4 cups. Add cloves, cinnamon and vinegar and simmer, uncovered, for 10 minutes. Add peaches; slowly heat for 5 minutes. Remove peaches and place with cut side up in a 3 quart ring mold which has been coated with mayonnaise to prevent sticking. Add hot water to make 1 2/3 cups. Add to lemon gelatin, stirring until dissolved; pour over peaches. Refrigerate until almost firm.

If using fresh cranberries and oranges, put through food chopper or food processor, using medium blade. Stir in sugar. Add hot water to gelatin, *stirring until dissolved; cool. Stir in cranberry-orange mixture. Pour over almost firm peach layer. Refrigerate until firm and unmold.*

Serve with Lemon-Cream Mayonnaise (below)

Lemon-Cream Mayonnaise:
1/2 cup mayonnaise
3 tablespoons lemon juice, or pineapple or orange juice
3 tablespoons confectioner's sugar
3 tablespoons heavy cream or 1/2 cup whipping cream, whipped.
dash of salt

Mix all together, and refrigerate until ready to use.

Makes 10 to 12 servings

Louise Dunn's Ginger Salad

1 16-ounce can white Queen Anne cherries, chopped
1 16-ounce can spiced peaches, cubed
orange juice or cooking sherry
1 small package lemon gelatin
1 small package orange gelatin
1/2 cup chopped pecans
1/2 cup crystalized ginger

Drain fruit, saving juices. Add orange juice or sherry to make 3 cups liquid. Heat to almost boiling and add gelatins, stirring well. Chill until almost syrupy. Add remainder of ingredients. Pour into 2 quart mold. Top with dressing when chilled, if desired.

Dressing:
1 egg yolk
1/4 cup honey or maple syrup
3/4 cup cream, whipped
juice of 1 lemon

Beat egg yolk well in top of double boiler. Add honey and cook for 1 minute or until thick. Cool and fold in cream; add lemon juice.

Aunt Blanche's Ribbon Salad

1 small package gelatin in your preference each: green, orange, yellow and red colors
4 cups hot water
2 cups cold water
2 cups milk
1 cup sugar
2 envelopes unflavored gelatin
1/2 cup cold water
1 pint sour cream
2 teaspoons vanilla

Dissolve each package of colored gelatin separately in 1 cup hot water. Add 1/2 cup cold water to each. Coat a 9 x 13 x 2 inch pan with mayonnaise and pour green colored gelatin into this pan. Set aside other colors. Bring to a boil 2 cups milk and add sugar, stirring until dissolved. In another dish dissolve the unflavored gelatin in 1/2 cup of cold water. Add this to milk and sugar mixture, mixing well. Add sour cream and vanilla, beating well; cool. Pour 1 1/2 cups of this white mixture on top of jelled green gelatin. When white mixture is firm, add orange gelatin. Repeat process for yellow gelatin, ending with the red gelatin on top.

Strawberry Aspic

1 can stewed tomatoes
2 tablespoons grated onion
3 tablespoons tarragon vinegar
2 shakes of Tabasco
1/2 teaspoon salt
1 small package strawberry gelatin

Blend tomatoes and onion in blender, add vinegar, Tabasco and salt. Bring to a full boil and stir in gelatin. Chill in molds or glass dish.

Serves 6

Note: You don't add any water to this. The tomatoes are juicy, and the onions and vinegar add plenty of liquid.

Nettie's Apricot Congealed Salad

1 small package lemon gelatin
1 large can apricots, drained and blended
pinch salt
juice of one lemon
juice of one orange
1 8-ounce package cream cheese
3/4 cup toasted nuts, chopped

Dissolve lemon gelatin in one cup boiling apricot juice. Add blended apricots, salt, lemon juice and orange juice. Form cream cheese and nuts into balls and place in center of individual molds that have been coated with mayonnaise. Pour gelatin over cream cheese and nut balls. Refrigerate.

Serves 6 to 8

A recipe from Mrs. East, one of the best cooks I have ever known. Everything she did was wonderful. I called one time and asked if she could bake me some cookies. She asked how many. When I told her 3,500 she screamed and said "not that many!" Several days later she called to tell me my cookies were ready.

Fruit Salad with Chutney

avocado, cut into pieces
orange, sectioned
grapefruit, sectioned
white grapes
Major Grey's chutney
lettuce

Arrange any portions you wish of avocado, oranges, grapefruit, and grapes in lettuce cups. Pour over each serving 1 generous teaspoon chutney. Serve with French dressing.

French Dressing:
1 clove garlic, crushed
1 teaspoon salt
1/2 teaspoon black pepper
1 teaspoon mustard
1 teaspoon sugar
2 pinches sweet basil
2 tablespoons vinegar
4 tablespoons olive oil

Crush garlic in bowl, mix with salt, pepper, mustard, sugar and basil (use powdered basil or powder the leaves between fingers). Then add vinegar and stir. Add olive oil and combine thoroughly.

Peach and Chutney Salad

fresh or canned peach halves
melted butter
chutney

Brush fresh or canned peach halves with melted butter in pan. Bake at 350 degrees for 10 minutes. Then fill halves with chutney and heat for 5 minutes.

Good with fowl or meat or as a dessert at lunch.

Frozen Fruit Salad

1 1/2 cups mayonnaise
12 ounces cream cheese, softened
2 tablespoons lemon rind, grated
1/4 cup powdered sugar
1 17-ounce can fruit cocktail, well drained
1 large banana, diced
2 cups fresh strawberries, sliced
2 cups fresh or frozen blueberries
2 cups heavy cream, whipped

Blend mayonnaise and cream cheese; add lemon rind, sugar, fruit cocktail, banana, strawberries and blueberries; fold in whipped cream; pour into ice cube trays and freeze. Cut into squares; serve on lettuce leaves.

Serves 8

Pineapple Slaw with Blue Cheese Dressing

4 cups cabbage, shredded
1 large carrot, shredded
1/2 cup radishes, sliced
1/2 cup green pepper, slivered
1 cup pineapple tidbits, well drained
3/4 cup buttermilk
3/4 cup mayonnaise
1/3 cup blue cheese, crumbled
1/2 teaspoon celery seed

Toss together cabbage, carrot, radishes, green pepper and pineapple tidbits. Combine buttermilk, mayonnaise, blue cheese and celery seed. Pour over cabbage mixture. Cover and chill well before serving.

Serves 6 to 8

Norma's Chunk Pickles

cucumbers
1 cup salt
boiling water
3 tablespoons powdered alum
5 pints vinegar
6 cups sugar

Slice cucumbers in chunk pieces and fill a gallon jar. Add salt and fill with boiling water. Let set for 6 days.

Pour off salt water and wash cucumbers. Replace in gallon jar and fill with boiling water. Let set for 24 hours.

Pour off water and add alum to cucumbers. Cover with boiling water. Let set for 24 hours.

Drain and place in jars. Mix vinegar and sugar. Bring to a boil and pour over cucumbers and seal.

Spring Dressing

1/4 cup chopped green onions
1/4 cup chopped parsley
1 clove garlic, grated
1 cup mayonnaise
1 tablespoon anchovy paste
1/2 cup thick sour cream
1/4 cup vinegar
1 tablespoon lemon juice
salt and pepper
1/4 teaspoon basil, optional

Add onions, parsley and garlic to mayonnaise. Mix anchovy paste with sour cream; add to mayonnaise. Thin with vinegar and lemon juice. Season with salt and pepper. Basil may be added if desired, especially when serving with tomatoes.

French Dressing a la Jarrell

1 small onion
1 small clove garlic
2 teaspoons sugar
1 teaspoon salt
1/3 cup wine vinegar
1/4 teaspoon cracked Java pepper (Spice Island)
1/4 teaspoon Beau Monde seasoning
1 tablespoon good sherry or bourbon
7/8 cup good olive oil

Cut up onion and garlic. Place in blender; add sugar and salt; blend to a paste. Add vinegar, pepper, Beau Monde and sherry; add olive oil slowly.

Will keep well.

Mick's Onion Confiture

1/4 pound unsalted butter
1 1/2 pounds medium white onions, sliced
(Vidalia onions when in season)
1 teaspoon salt
1 1/2 teaspoons ground pepper, fresh
2/3 cup sugar
6 tablespoons wine or sherry vinegar
2 tablespoons grenadine or red currant jelly
1 cup red wine

Heat butter in skillet until light brown. Add onions, salt, pepper and sugar. Stir well, continue cooking over lower heat for 30 minutes, stirring occasionally.

Add remaining ingredients, and continue cooking, uncovered, for 30 minutes or more, stirring often. Mixture should bubble slowly. Confiture is done when it is the consistency of jam.

Good served as an accompaniment with meat.

Brandy Sauce

1/3 cup butter
1 cup sifted powdered sugar
3 tablespoons brandy
3 egg yolks, beaten
1/2 cup cream

Melt butter in double boiler. Gradually add sugar. Slowly beat in brandy, one tablespoon at a time, then add egg yolks and cream. Cook until slightly thickened.

Seafood Cocktail Sauce

3/4 cup chili sauce
2 tablespoons horseradish, drained
2 teaspoons lemon juice
3 drops Tabasco sauce

Blend above ingredients and serve with chilled shrimp or seafood. Also makes a delicious dip for fried shrimp or fish sticks.

Ninth Street House Entrance

Chicken a la Jerusalem

2 pounds of chicken, cut in serving pieces
1 cup flour
1/4 pound butter
salt, pepper, nutmeg
1/2 pound sliced mushrooms
6 fresh or frozen artichoke hearts, cooked
1/2 cup cream sherry
whipping cream
minced parsley
minced chives

Dredge chicken in flour, then brown in butter. Season with salt, pepper, and nutmeg. Add mushrooms and artichokes. Pour sherry over all. Cover and simmer for 15 minutes, or until tender and most of wine has evaporated. Stir in cream to desired consistency. Top with minced parsley and chives.

Honey'd Chicken

1/4 cup butter or margarine
1/4 cup honey
1/4 cup prepared mustard
1 teaspoon salt
1 teaspoon curry powder
1 three pound broiler/fryer, cut into serving pieces

Melt butter over moderately low heat. Add honey, mustard, salt and curry powder. Roll chicken in mixture and arrange single layer in buttered baking dish. Bake at 350 degrees for one hour or until tender. Baste chicken occasionally.

Serves 4

Parmesan Baked Chicken

4 1/2 cups fresh bread crumbs
1 1/4 cups grated Parmesan cheese
1 teaspoon salt
1/3 cup chopped parsley
1 1/2 cups butter, melted
3 cloves garlic, crushed
1 tablespoon Dijon mustard
2 teaspoons Worcestershire sauce
3 2 1/2 to 3-pound fryers, cut up

Mix together bread crumbs, cheese, salt and parsley. Spread in shallow pan. Melt butter, add garlic, mustard and Worcestershire sauce. Stir well. Dip chicken into butter mixture, then roll in crumb mixture. Bake at 325 degrees 1 to 1 1/2 hours. Serve warm or room temperature.

Serves 10 to 12

Breast of Chicken en Croûte

1 whole boneless breast of chicken
1/4 cup clarified butter
2 sheets phyllo dough
1 egg, beaten
1 3/4-ounce Boursin Cheese Stuffing (see below)

Cut chicken breast in half and sear in hot clarified butter. Place one sheet of phyllo dough on parchment paper and lightly brush with clarified butter. Cut dough in half and place equal amounts of cheese stuffing, centered, on each side of dough. Place chicken breast on top of stuffing. Fold each side lengthwise and roll up. Brush with egg wash. Bake at 350 degrees for approximately 25 to 30 minutes or until golden brown.

Boursin Cheese Stuffing:
3 ounces Boursin cheese
1 ounce butter
1 1/2 ounces chopped pecans

Mix all together and set aside.

Chicken Breast with Raspberry Vinegar Sauce

6 chicken breast halves, skinned and boned
1 tablespoon oil
1 tablespoon butter
1/2 cup raspberry vinegar
1 cup chicken broth
3/4 cup whipping cream
1/4 cup toasted, chopped, slivered almonds
2 tablespoons finely chopped fresh parsley

Pound chicken breasts slightly to make even in thickness. Heat oil and butter in skillet. Add chicken breasts and brown all sides until golden and remove. Drain pan of excess fat, then deglaze with vinegar and chicken broth. Return chicken breasts to pan and simmer, covered, for 20 minutes. Remove chicken and place on serving platter. Keep warm. Reduce pan juices to 1/4 to 1/3 cup. This will probably take quite a while. Then add whipping cream. Reduce pan liquids to 1/2 volume (at least 10 minutes). Pour resulting sauce over chicken breasts. Garnish with almonds and fresh parsley.

Chicken Breasts with Orange and Green Peppercorn Sauce

3 whole chicken breasts, cut in half, skinned and boned
1/2 cup flour
1 tablespoon seasoned salt
1 teaspoon Hungarian sweet paprika
2 tablespoons butter
2 tablespoons oil
1/2 cup water
1/2 cup orange flavored liqueur
1/2 cup dry or semi-dry white wine
1/2 orange, sliced
1 tablespoon green peppercorns
1/2 teaspoon salt
1/4 teaspoon dry tarragon, muddled

Dredge chicken in flour, salt and paprika. In skillet, heat butter and oil. Sauté chicken quickly on both sides (about 6 minutes total). Remove to sprayed baking dish. Deglaze skillet mixture with water; reduce liquid to 1/2 volume. Add orange liqueur, white wine, sliced oranges, peppercorns, salt and tarragon. Continue cooking and stirring. Sauté for 3 minutes. Pour over browned chicken and cover with foil. (May be refrigerated at this stage) Bake, covered, at 350 degrees for 20 minutes; uncover and bake for an additional 10 minutes.

Chicken Cantonese

1 fat hen (5 pound hen or 2 fryers)
2 cups rice
2 cans mushroom soup
1 can mushrooms, drained
4 tablespoons minced red pimento
1 tablespoon minced onion
2 eggs slightly beaten
salt and pepper to taste
2 cups dried bread crumbs

Cover hen wih salted water and stew until tender. Let it cool in broth. Skim off fat and reserve. Remove chicken from bowl, skin and bone and cut in small pieces. Wash rice and cook in chicken broth. Add the soup, mushrooms, pimento, onion, eggs, salt and pepper. Combine with chicken and pour in greased baking dish. Heat the fat in skillet and saute´ bread crumbs. Mix thoroughly and spread over chicken and rice mixture. Bake in moderate oven 1 to 1 1/2 hours.

Serves 12

Chicken in Phyllo

24 sheets phyllo dough
2/3 cups butter
12 chicken breast halves, skinned and boned
salt and pepper
Parmesan cheese

Brush phyllo sheet lightly with butter. Season and dip each chicken breast in sauce (below) and place on a sheet, top with second sheet of phyllo dough and wrap up envelope style. Brush top with butter and sprinkle with Parmesan cheese. Repeat with each chicken breast piece. Bake in ungreased pan at 375 degrees for 30 minutes.

Dipping sauce:
3/4 cup chopped green onions, including tops
3/4 cup mayonnaise
3 tablespoons lemon juice
3 small cloves garlic, minced
1/2 teaspoon dry tarragon

Mix all ingredients together. Serve with Mornay Sauce.

Mornay Sauce:
1 stick butter
1 small bunch chopped green onions
2 tablespoons flour
1 pint half and half

1/2 cup finely chopped parsley
1/2 pound grated Monterey Jack cheese
1 tablespoon sherry
cayenne pepper
salt

Melt butter in skillet, add onions and sauté. Stir in flour until well blended. Add cream, parsley and cheese. Heat and stir over low temperature until cheese is melted. Sauce can be used to accompany chicken and as a garnish for asparagus or broccoli.

Mexican Torte

3 pounds ground beef, browned and drained
3 cups chunky type salsa
1/2 cup sliced green olives
1/2 cup sliced green onion
1 package 10 inch flour tortillas
1 cup melted butter or margarine
12 to 15 slices cheddar cheese
12 to 15 slices Monterey Jack cheese
3 or 4 tomatoes, sliced, reserving one
2 cups sour cream

Combine ground beef, salsa, olives and green onion in a mixing bowl. Set aside.

Place first tortilla on greased baking sheet that has at least 1 inch sides. Brush butter on tortilla then spread about 1 1/2 cups of the beef mixture on the tortilla. Spread to edges, then top with slices of cheddar and Monterey Jack cheese, and slices of tomato. Butter second tortilla on both sides, then place on top. Repeat layering beef mixture, cheeses and tomato until you have five to six layers. Place last tortilla on top with cheeses only. Bake at 350 degrees for 35 to 40 minutes or until heated through.

If torte begins to brown too much, cover loosely with foil. Slices of tomato can be placed on top during the last five minutes. When baked, let sit before slicing and garnishing with sour cream.

Orange Ginger Pork Chops

6 one-inch pork chops
1/4 cup orange juice
1/2 teaspoon salt
1 teaspoon ground ginger
6 orange slices (one large orange)
3 tablespoons cornstarch
3/4 cup dairy sour cream

In a skillet coated with vegetable cooking spray, brown chops well over medium heat about 10 minutes per side. Add orange juice, cover and simmer about 30 minutes.

Uncover, sprinkle chops with salt and ginger and top each with an orange slice. Cover and cook 10 to 15 minutes more or until chops are fork tender. Remove chops to an oven proof platter and top each with sour cream. Place under broiler about one minute. Serve immediately.

Serves 6

Sweet and Sour Pork

2 pounds lean pork, cut into 1/2 inch cubes
1/4 cup vegetable oil
1 cup chicken stock
2 green peppers, cut into eighths
1 cup pineapple chunks, drained
3 tablespoons flour
2 tablespoons soy sauce
1/2 cup vinegar
1/2 cup sugar
1/2 teaspoon salt
1/4 teaspoon black pepper

Brown pork in vegetable oil. Do not let pieces of pork touch when browning. Remove pork from skillet as it browns. Drain skillet, place pork back into skillet. Add stock, green peppers, pineapple chunks, flour which has been mixed with soy sauce and vinegar, sugar, salt and pepper. Simmer 15 minutes.

Serve hot over cooked rice.

Serves 6

Blue Cheese Stuffed Pork Chops

1 stick butter
1 large onion, chopped
1 cup mushrooms, sliced
1/4 pound blue cheese, crumbled
croutons or dry bread crumbs
salt and pepper to taste
6 one-inch pork chops, cut with pocket

Melt butter; sauté onion and mushrooms in butter. Remove from heat. Stir in crumbled blue cheese. Add enough croutons or bread crumbs to absorb moisture. Mix well and stuff into chops. Bake uncovered, at 350 degrees for one hour or until done. Baste with drippings occasionally while cooking.

Serves 6

People in western Kentucky or the entire state never tire of country ham. We can travel 60 miles north into Southern Illinois and the guests like it but they don't fall into the floor and kick. I had bought a very good ham in the country, with white streaks, and prepared it for a party in the north. I served it sliced on a silver tray and beautifully garnished. A man came up to me and said, "That is the best corned-beef I ever put into my mouth." I could not tell him the difference.

Norma's Salmon Patties

1 15-ounce can salmon
1 tablespoon prepared mustard
1 egg
1/2 cup onion, chopped medium fine
2 tablespoons plain flour
salt and pepper to taste
1 cup cracker crumbs, about 24 -26 soda crackers

Mix all ingredients well, breaking up salmon and mashing any soft bone pieces. Heat shortening or 1/4 inch of cooking oil in skillet on medium heat. Dip about 1/2 cup salmon mixture in cracker crumbs, working in a small amount of crumbs. Coat with crumbs again and shape into patties about 1/2 inch thick. Gently place in heated oil. Cook until golden brown on both sides. Grease should not be hot enough to start browning, so as not to soak up grease. Remove from skillet and drain on paper towels.

Sole Poached in Vermouth

6 large fillets of sole
1 1/4 cups dry vermouth
4 egg yolks
1/4 pound butter, cut up
3 tablespoons heavy cream
salt

Arrange fillets in large skillet and pour vermouth to cover fish. Bring to a boiling point, then reduce the heat and poach for 10 minutes per measured inch of thickness of the fish – until just cooked through. Remove fillets to baking dish and keep warm.

Reduce remaining liquid in frying pan and heat on high until it is practically a glaze.

Put egg yolks and pieces of butter in top of double boiler over hot water. Beat with whisk until smooth and thick, then beat in cream and reduce liquid and add salt to taste. Do not let water boil or eggs will curdle. Pour sauce over fillets and brown quickly under broiler.

Serves 6

Olive's Shrimp de Jonghe

2 pounds shrimp, cooked, shelled and deveined
1 cup dry bread crumbs
1 cup melted butter
1 cup dry sherry
2 cloves garlic, crushed
1/3 teaspoon dried tarragon leaves, crushed
1/3 teaspoon chervil
1 teaspoon parsley, chopped
1 tablespoon onion, chopped
pinch salt
pinch thyme
pinch mace
pinch nutmeg
dash black pepper

Place shrimp in four individual buttered serving dishes. Combine bread crumbs, butter, sherry and seasonings. Layer bread crumbs over shrimp. Bake at 325 degrees for approximately 30 minutes.

Serve with lots of French bread, tossed salad and white wine.

Charles' Fish in a Corn Bed

Prepare a corn bread using a recipe that calls for cream style corn. (Cooking with Curtis Grace, page 78)

Season and bake fish fillets until almost done. Bake corn bread until almost done. Place fillets on top of corn bread and spoon some of corn bread over fillets and continue baking until done. Cut in squares and serve.

Good served with cole slaw.

Crab and Shrimp Au Gratin over Puff Pastry

Seasoning mix:
1 tablespoon + 1/2 teaspoon salt
1 1/2 teaspoons onion powder
1 1/2 teaspoons garlic powder
3/4 tablespoon dry mustard
3/4 teaspoon cayenne pepper
3/4 teaspoon paprika
3/4 teaspoon dried basil leaves
1/2 teaspoon white pepper
1/2 teaspoon black pepper

Combine all ingredients, mixing well. Store in airtight container.

Au gratin sauce:
2 1/2 tablespoons unsalted butter
1/3 cup finely chopped onions
1 teaspoon seasoning mix
4 teaspoons flour
1 1/2 cups milk
1/2 cup heavy cream
1 1/4 cups cheddar cheese, grated
1 bay leaf

In a 2 quart saucepan combine butter and onions, sauté over high heat about 1 minute, stirring frequently. Stir in seasoning mix and cook for 1 minute longer, stirring well. Gradually stir in flour and milk. Bring mixture to a quick simmer and whisk frequently. Add cream and bring to a boil, whisking constantly, until thickened. Remove from heat and stir in cheese until melted; add bay leaf and set aside.

Shrimp and crab preparation:

4 1/2 tablespoons unsalted butter
3/4 pound peeled medium shrimp
3/4 pound lump crabmeat
1 teaspoon seasoning mix
2 tablespoons + 1 teaspoon white wine
1/3 cup chopped green onions
2 tablespoons Parmesan cheese, finely grated

In large skillet, melt butter, add shrimp and sauté until plump, about 1 minute. Stir in crabmeat, seasoning mix, wine and onions. Cook about 1 minute, stirring occasionally. Add Parmesan, drain off the cooking sauce and set aside. Add seafood mixture to au gratin sauce and remove bay leaf. Now return some of the cooking sauce to the au gratin, thinning to your own preference.

Serve over puff pastry.

Stuffed Fillet of Sole

1 cup cracker crumbs
1/4 cup chopped celery
1/4 cup chopped onion
2 tablespoons chopped green pepper
1/4 cup melted butter
1/4 cup crabmeat
1/3 cup small shrimp
1 egg
1/2 teaspoon dry mustard
1/2 teaspoon cayenne pepper
6 fillets of sole (use Petrale sole if available)

Sauce:
2/3 cup mayonnaise
2/3 cup sour cream
1 1/2 tablespoons lemon juice
paprika
parsley sprigs

Combine cracker crumbs, celery, onion, green pepper, butter, crabmeat, shrimp, egg, mustard and cayenne pepper together and mix lightly with a fork. Divide stuffing into 6 portions and place in center of each fillet. Lap each end of fish over center portion at an angle. (No need to use toothpicks or tie as they hold together very nicely. May be refrigerated at this point to bake later.) Arrange in a lightly buttered baking dish. Bake at 350 *degrees for 20 minutes. Prepare sauce while sole is baking by combining ingredients and mixing well. After the 20 minutes are over, remove sole from oven and spread sauce mixture on top. Return to oven for 5 to 10 minutes. Do not overheat as sour cream may curdle. Remove and garnish with paprika and parsley sprigs.*

Schroeder - Grace Houses

Toots Smith's Broccoli Mold

2 packages chopped frozen broccoli
1 1/2 envelopes unflavored gelatin
1 cup beef bouillon
1 3-ounce package cream cheese, softened
1 hard boiled egg, grated
1/2 to 3/4 cup mayonnaise
dash Tabasco sauce
1 tablespoon Worcestershire sauce
1 tablespoon onion, grated
salt and pepper to taste

Cook broccoli according to directions. Drain well. Sprinkle gelatin over beef bouillon and heat to dissolve. Add cream cheese to bouillon mixture, stirring to blend. Add broccoli, grated eggs, mayonnaise, Tabasco, Worcestershire, onion and seasonings. Place in mold that has been coated with mayonnaise. Chill until firm.

Good served as salad or cold vegetable.

Serves 6 to 8

Jane's Potatoes Niçoise

1 clove garlic
3 medium potatoes (1 pound)
3 large medium-ripe tomatoes, peeled
boiling water
3 red onions, sliced
1/4 teaspoon dried tarragon leaves
1/4 teaspoon dried basil leaves
1 1/2 tablespoons parsley, chopped
2 teaspoons salt
1/4 teaspoon nutmeg
2 tablespoons butter
1/2 cup cheddar or Gruyère cheese, grated

Rub baking dish with garlic. Pare potatoes and slice 1/4 inch thick. Scald tomatoes in boiling water. Peel and slice 1/2 inch thick. Slice onions thin. Layer potatoes, onions and tomatoes in baking dish with tomatoes last. Combine herbs and seasonings. Sprinkle over top. Dot with butter. Cover and bake at 400 degrees for 45 minutes. Uncover. Sprinkle with cheese and bake 15 minutes longer.

Nat's Mushroom Ring

1 pound fresh mushrooms
5 tablespoons butter, divided
2 tablespoons onion, finely chopped
3/4 teaspoon salt
1/4 teaspoon ground nutmeg
1/4 teaspoon ground ginger
4 tablespoons all-purpose flour
1/2 cup milk
3 dashes Tabasco
2 large eggs, well beaten

Wash mushrooms gently under cold running water and dry on paper towels. Do not peel unless skin is brown. Chop mushrooms coarsely. In an 8-cup glass container, melt 4 tablespoons butter. Add chopped mushrooms and onions and cook until vegetables are tender. Add seasonings and flour, blend. Add milk and Tabasco and cook until mixture thickens. (You may prepare recipe to this point in the morning or evening the day before serving, refrigerate, and bake when ready to serve.)

Add well beaten eggs to mushroom mixture and spoon into a 1-quart soufflé or casserole buttered with remaining tablespoon of butter. Bake at 350 degrees until set. If a ring mold is used, fill with green peas after it has been gently turned out onto a warm serving tray.

Zucchini Tomato Pie

2 cups chopped zucchini
1 cup chopped tomato
1/2 cup chopped onion
1/3 cup grated Parmesan cheese
1 1/2 cups milk
3/4 cup biscuit mix
3 eggs
1/2 teaspoon salt
1/4 teaspoon pepper

Mix all ingredients and pour into a greased pie plate. Bake at 325 degrees for 30 to 40 minutes.

Serves 6

Shredded Beets with Tarragon

5 medium-sized raw beets
1/4 to 1/3 cup butter
2 to 3 tablespoons tarragon vinegar
1 teaspoon fresh tarragon
(or 1/2 teaspoon dried tarragon)
1 small clove garlic, peeled
salt and pepper to taste
1 teaspoon sugar

Wash and scrub beets but do not peel. Shred raw beets, using coarse grater or processor. Melt butter. Add vinegar and tarragon. Stick a toothpick in garlic clove and drop in pan. Add shredded raw beets, a dash of salt and pepper and stir to combine. Cover pan and simmer 8 to 15 minutes, just until tender and crisp. Stir several times during cooking to combine ingredients. Instead, you may microwave on high power for 5 to 6 minutes. Remove from heat, take out garlic clove on toothpick, add sugar and stir. Taste again and adjust seasonings.

Serves 4 to 6

Baked Eggplant

1 medium eggplant
salt water
1 can tomato soup
1 finely chopped onion
1 finely chopped green pepper
celery seed
dash curry powder
1 tablespoon butter
salt
red pepper
2 eggs, hard boiled and chopped
cracker crumbs
cream

Peel eggplant, then cut into pieces and boil in salt water until tender. Mash fine. Cook tomato soup, onion, green pepper, celery seed, curry powder, butter, salt, and red pepper in skillet. When thick, add eggplant and hard boiled eggs. Pour into buttered baking dish. Top with cracker crumbs and a little cream.

Bake at 325 degrees until hot and bubbly and crumbs are browned.

Serves 6

Oven Fried Eggplant

1 medium eggplant
1/4 cup mayonnaise
1/4 cup grated Parmesan cheese
1/2 cup soda crackers, crushed fine

Slice eggplant into 1/2 inch thick slices, but do not peel. Spread mayonnaise in thin layer on both sides of eggplant slices. Mix cheese and cracker crumbs and coat eggplant. Place slices in single layer on baking sheet which has been sprayed with cooking spray.

Bake at 425 degrees. After 10 minutes, turn and continue baking for 5 minutes or until browned and tender. Serve with Yogurt Dressing (optional) or lemon wedges.

Yogurt Dressing:
1 cup unflavored yogurt
1/2 cup sour cream
1/2 teaspoon onion powder
juice of 1/2 lemon (about 1 tablespoon)
dash garlic powder

Combine all ingredients and mix well.

Serves 6

Stewed Green Beans with Tomato and Mint

2 cups finely chopped onion
1/3 cup olive oil
4 large garlic cloves, minced
2 tablespoons dried mint, crumbled
1 28-ounce can plum tomatoes, drained and chopped
juice from tomatoes
salt and pepper to taste
2 pounds green beans, trimmed

In skillet, cook onion in oil over moderately low heat, stirring occasionally until softened; add garlic and mint. Cook mixture, stirring constantly, for 2 minutes. Add tomatoes and tomato juice, salt and pepper to taste. Simmer for 15 minutes, stirring occasionally. Add beans and simmer, covered, stirring occasionally, for 30 minutes or until beans are very tender.

Beans improve in flavor if made at least 1 day and up to 3 days in advance, cooled to room temperature, and kept covered and chilled. Serve beans at room temperature or heated.

Serves 6 to 8

Spanish Rice

1 medium green pepper, chopped
1 small onion, chopped
3 tablespoons oil
1 cup long grain rice, uncooked
2 cups canned tomatoes
2 cups water
salt and pepper to taste

Over medium heat, sauté pepper and onion in oil. Add rice and cook until golden brown, stirring frequently. Add tomatoes, water, salt and pepper. Cover pan and simmer over low heat until water is absorbed.

Serves 6 to 8

Bulgar Pilaf

3/4 cup finely chopped onion
2 tablespoons unsalted butter
1 cup bulgar (cracked wheat)
1 teaspoon freshly grated orange rind
1/4 cup raisins
1 3/4 cup canned chicken broth
salt
pepper
6 tablespoons pine nuts, toasted lightly
1/4 cup minced fresh parsley leaves
1/4 cup thinly sliced scallion greens

In saucepan, cook onion in butter, stirring until softened. Stir in bulgar and orange rind. Cook mixture for 1 minute. Add raisins, broth, salt and pepper to taste. Bring to boil and cook, covered, over low heat for 10 to 15 minutes, or until liquid is absorbed.

Fluff with fork and let cook for 15 minutes. May be prepared up to this point 6 hours in advance and kept chilled, covered loosely, until 30 minutes before serving. Fluff pilaf with fork and stir in pine nuts and parsley and scallion greens.

Serves 5 to 6

Cracked Wheat Pilaf

1 cup cracked wheat
1/4 cup finely chopped onion
1 tablespoon oil
2 cups chicken broth

Sauté wheat and onions in oil to toast wheat, but not brown onion. Add broth and bring to boil; stir, reduce heat, cover and simmer until all liquid is absorbed, about 20 to 30 minutes. Fluff with fork and leave uncovered to dry slightly before serving. Pilaf should not be stirred with a wooden spoon as this mushes cereal.

Serves 4 to 6

Three of our four sons are married and it has all taken place at the "Ninth Street House" on a Sunday so Norma and I could attend.

Miriam's Marinated Vegetables

1 large can sliced mushrooms
1 can water chestnuts, sliced
1 small can pitted ripe olives, sliced
1 small can stuffed olives, sliced
1 large can artichoke hearts, cut up
1 large can Italian green beans
4 green onions, sliced
seasoned salt
1/2 cup cider vinegar
1/3 cup oil
2 tablespoons dill weed
1/2 cup sugar

Drain all vegetables. Make 3 layers in any order. Sprinkle each layer with seasoned salt. Combine vinegar, oil, dill weed and sugar. Pour over vegetables and marinate in refrigerator for 24 hours.

Serves 10 to 12

Poulston's Rice Casserole

1 box Rice-a-Roni, chicken flavored
2 green onions, chopped
1/2 green pepper, chopped
8 to 10 stuffed olives, chopped
1 package slivered almonds
1 jar marinated artichokes, chopped and drained
liquid from artichokes
1/2 cup Hellman's mayonnaise
1 teaspoon curry powder

Prepare Rice-a-Roni as directed on package. Add green onions, green pepper, olives, almonds and artichokes. Add the liquid from artichokes to mayonnaise, add to rice mixture, blend well and stir in curry powder. Bake in buttered casserole dish at 350 degrees for 15 to 30 minutes. This dish is good served warm or cold.

Serves 6 to 8

Chilie Relleno Casserole

1 3-ounce can whole green chilies
6 eggs
3/4 cup evaporated milk
salt and pepper
3 cups of Monterey Jack or cheddar cheese

Wash and seed peppers, cut into strips, and place in greased 8 x 8 inch casserole. Beat eggs; add milk and seasonings. Spread cheese on chilies; pour egg mixture over. Bake at 350 degrees for 35 to 40 minutes.

Serves 6

Seafood Casserole

1 stick butter
1 cup celery, chopped
1 cup green pepper, chopped
1 pound mushrooms, chopped
1 cup onions, chopped
2 pounds shrimp, cooked
1 can crabmeat
1/2 pound sharp cheese, grated
1/2 cup wild rice, cooked
1/2 cup white rice, cooked
4 tablespoons butter
4 tablespoons flour
2 cups milk
salt and pepper to taste

Melt butter and sauté celery, green pepper, mushrooms and onions. Add shrimp, crabmeat, cheese and rice. Make cream sauce of butter, flour and milk. Add ingredients to cream sauce. Correct seasonings. Place in buttered casserole. Bake at 325 degrees for 45 minutes.

Serves 10 to 12

Janet's Eggplant Casserole

sliced eggplant, unpeeled
sliced onions, uniform in size to eggplant
Mozzarella cheese, grated
can of tomato sauce

Layer bottom of ovenproof casserole with ingredients in order listed. Bake at 350 degrees for 15 to 20 minutes, or as Janet says "until you are ready to eat –1 Scotch –2 Scotches, whatever it takes!"

Sausage Rice Casserole
by Maxine Hearell

2 pounds pork sausage

1 cup bell pepper, finely chopped
3/4 cup onion, chopped
2 1/2 cups celery, coarsely chopped
2 small packages instant chicken noodle soup
4 1/2 cups boiling water
1 cup rice, uncooked
1/2 teaspoon salt
1 cup blanched almonds, optional
1/4 cup butter, melted

Brown sausage, pour off excess fat. Add bell pepper, onion and one cup of celery to sausage and sauté. Set aside. In a large pan add soup mix to boiling water, stir in rice, cover and simmer for 20 minutes or until tender. Add sausage mixture and salt, stirring well. Pour into buttered baking dish and sprinkle remaining celery and almonds over the top. Drizzle with melted butter. Bake uncovered at 325 degrees for 30 minutes.

Serves 12 to 14

Spinach and Artichoke Casserole

1 pound spinach
frozen or canned artichokes
3 slices bacon
1/2 cup chopped onion
1 tablespoon flour
1 clove garlic, minced
3 scallions, chopped
1/3 cup heavy cream
salt and pepper, to taste
bread crumbs
butter

Cook and chop spinach; extract all water and set aside. If using frozen artichokes, cook and chop; set aside. Fry bacon until crisp, crumble and set aside. Pour off all but 1 tablespoon of bacon fat. Add onion to remaining bacon fat and cook until tender. Add flour, garlic, and scallions. Stir in cream. Cook until thickened. Add spinach, chopped artichokes, and bacon to sauce. Season with salt and pepper.

Pour into buttered baking dish. Sprinkle with bread crumbs and dot with butter. Bake at 400 degrees until nicely browned, 10 to 15 minutes.

Serves 4

Tuna Casserole

3 cans cut green asparagus, drained
3 cans white tuna, solid packed, flaked
6 hard boiled eggs, sliced
3 cans mushroom soup, undiluted
American cheese, grated
butter
cayenne pepper

Layer ingredients above in buttered casserole in order listed. Top with cheese. Dot with butter and dust with pepper.

Bake at 325 degrees until bubbly hot. Serve over toast.

Serves 8 to 12

Hot Turkey Casserole

1 to 1 1/2 cups cooked turkey, chopped
1/2 cup Kraft mayonnaise
1/2 can cream of chicken soup
1/2 can cream of mushroom soup
2 chopped hard boiled eggs
1/2 cup toasted sliced almonds
1/2 teaspoon minced onion
1 can water chestnuts, drained
1/3 cup bread crumbs

Mix all ingredients except bread crumbs thoroughly. Place in greased casserole and top with crumbs. Bake at 350 degrees for 20 minutes.

Serves 6

Zucchini Casserole

3 cups grated zucchini
1/2 cup oil
1 cup biscuit mix
4 eggs
1/2 cup chopped onion
salt
pepper
bread crumbs
grated cheese

Combine all ingredients except crumbs and cheese. Mix well and place in greased casserole. Top with bread crumbs. Cover, and bake at 350 degrees for 25 to 30 minutes. Remove cover and put cheese on top. Return to oven and bake for 5 to 10 minutes more.

Serves 6

Mrs. Dobson's Noodle and Swiss Cheese Casserole

1 8-ounce package medium noodles, cooked and drained
1/2 pound Swiss cheese, grated
1 tablespoon onion juice
1 teaspoon Worcestershire sauce
1/4 cup melted butter
1 pint sour cream
1/2 cup bread crumbs

Add cheese to hot noodles. Add onion juice, Worcestershire sauce, and butter. Cool. Add sour cream. Top with bread crumbs and bake at 350 degrees for 1 hour.

Mrs. Dobson remarks,
"This is delicious. I've used it over at The Center."
(Jewish Center in Union City, Tennessee.)

Fish Pudding From Calvary Church

3 pounds red snapper
  or other favorite fish
3 eggs, beaten
1 cup milk
1 stick butter, melted
1 cup cracker crumbs
1 tablespoon parsley, chopped
1 tablespoon onion, grated
juice of one lemon
salt and pepper to taste
sherry to taste

Bake fish with a little seasoning. Bone and flake. Place in a bowl and add eggs, mixing well. Add milk and one half of the butter, one half of the cracker crumbs, parsley, onion, lemon juice, salt, pepper and sherry. Mix, then place in buttered baking dish. Top with remaining cracker crumbs and butter. If mixture appears to be dry, add a little more milk. Place baking dish in pan of hot water and bake at 325 degrees for 50 minutes. Serve with tartar sauce.

Serves 8 to 10

The ladies of Calvary in Memphis, Tn. serve lunch throughout Lent. This is one dish they can never make enough of to feed to their guests, says Carol Gardner!

Purcell - Fitzpatrick House

Strawberry Shortcake

Your favorite pie pastry recipe, or a frozen pie shell brought to room temperature
butter, melted
sugar
fresh or frozen strawberries, or another fruit
whipped cream or topping

Prepare your favorite pie pastry recipe and roll it as thin as possible. It does not have to look uniform. Place on a cookie sheet, prick with a fork, brush with melted butter and sprinkle with sugar. Tilt cookie sheet to side and tap on bottom to remove excess sugar. Bake at 325 degrees until brown. Cool, then break or cut into pieces and layer individual servings with freshly sliced, sweetened strawberries, peaches or your favorite fruit. Top with whipped cream or a dairy topping.

So good it makes you want to slap your grandmother.

Easy Winter Apricot Pie

2 cups dried apricots
1 cup orange juice
pastry for two pie crusts, your favorite recipe
1 tablespoon cornstarch
1/2 cup light brown sugar, firmly packed
1/4 teaspoon salt
1 tablespoon butter

Soak apricots in orange juice for 2 hours. While apricots are soaking, prepare your recipe for pie crusts. Line an 8 inch pie plate with crust and let chill.

After 2 hours, drain apricots, reserving 2/3 cup of liquid. Heat cornstarch, brown sugar, and salt in saucepan. Gradually stir in the reserved orange juice. Cook mixture over moderate heat until slightly thickened, stirring constantly.

Spread apricots around crust, pour the syrup over them and dot with butter. Cover with lattice pastry top or plain slit top and bake at 400 degrees for 12 minutes. Reduce heat to 325 degrees and bake for 20 minutes or until pastry is golden brown.

Judy's Chess Pie with Raisins and Nuts

1/2 cup butter
1 cup sugar
3 egg yolks, beaten
1 egg white, stiffly beaten
1 cup raisins
1 cup chopped nuts
1 teaspoon vanilla

Cream butter and sugar; add beaten egg yolks and stiffly beaten egg white. Mix well and add raisins, nuts and vanilla. Bake at 400 degrees until filling is set. Reduce heat to 350 degrees and bake until brown. Serve with whipped cream.

Note: To make a full pie, add an extra egg and a hand full more raisins and nuts.

Rhubarb Pie

1 pound frozen or fresh rhubarb
1/2 cup butter, melted
1 1/2 cups sugar
3 tablespoons flour
1/2 teaspoon nutmeg
pastry for 2 pie crusts

Thaw frozen rhubarb and mix with butter, sugar, flour and nutmeg.

Place into unbaked pie shell, then top with remaining pastry. Brush with butter and sprinkle with sugar. Bake at 350 degrees for 45 minutes to 1 hour or until brown.

Serves 6

Coconut Crunch Pie

4 egg whites
pinch of salt
1 cup sugar
1 teaspoon vanilla
1 cup graham cracker crumbs
1/2 cup coconut
1/2 cup pecans

Beat egg whites at high speed of electric mixer until stiff. Add salt, gradually add sugar and fold in vanilla. Stir in graham cracker crumbs, coconut, and pecans. Pour into a well-buttered pie pan and bake at 350 degrees for 20 minutes.

Serve with whipped cream or sliced bananas and whipped cream.

Sour Cream and Raisin Pie

4 egg yolks
2 cups sour cream
2 cups sugar
4 teaspoons flour
2 cups raisins
4 egg whites
8 teaspoons sugar, for meringue
1 9-inch baked pastry shell

Put yolks in saucepan and add sour cream, sugar, flour and raisins. Mix well and cook until thick. Pour into a 9-inch baked pie shell. Beat egg whites with mixer and add 8 teaspoons sugar to form meringue. Spread meringue on top of pie and bake at 400 degrees until brown.

Meringue Pie

3 egg whites
1/4 teaspoon cream of tartar
1 cup sugar
18 soda crackers, finely crushed
1/2 cup pecans
1/2 pint whipping cream, whipped
1/2 cup apricot preserves
3 tablespoons brandy

Beat egg whites and cream of tartar until fluffy. Slowly add sugar; fold in cracker crumbs and pecans. Press into a well-greased 9 inch pie pan and bake at 325 degrees for 30 minutes. Cool. Top with whipped cream mixed with preserves and brandy.

Hershey Bar Pie

6 small Hershey bars with almonds
17 marshmallows, quartered
1/2 cup milk
1 cup cream, whipped
graham cracker crust

Melt Hershey bars, marshmallows and milk in top of double boiler. Let cool, then add whipped cream. Pour into a 9 inch graham cracker crust and place in refrigerator. Serve with a small amount of shaved or slivered bitter chocolate on top of each piece.

Serves 6

Miss Elva's Ozark Pudding

3/4 cup sugar
1 egg, beaten
3 heaping tablespoons plain flour
1 1/4 teaspoons baking powder
1/2 cup pecans or black walnuts, chopped
1/2 cup apples, peeled and chopped
pinch salt
1 teaspoon vanilla

Add sugar to beaten egg. Combine flour, baking powder, nuts, apples, salt and vanilla with sugar and egg mixture. Pour into well greased 8" x 8" baking dish. Bake at 325 degrees for 40 minutes. Serve warm with vanilla ice cream.

Serves 6

Apricot Nectar Cake

1 package plain yellow cake mix
3/4 cup cooking oil
1 small package lemon gelatin
2 teaspoons lemon juice
3/4 cup apricot nectar
4 eggs, separated

In mixing bowl combine cake mix, oil, gelatin, lemon juice, apricot nectar and egg yolks, one at a time, beating well after each addition. In another bowl, beat whites until stiff. With spatula, gently fold egg whites into cake batter. Pour mixture into well greased and floured tube pan. Bake at 325 degrees for 45 minutes to 1 hour or until cake tests done.

Icing:
1/2 cup orange juice
2 cups powdered sugar

Mix together ingredients for icing, making a glaze. Spoon over cake when cool.

Cherry Chocolate Cake

1 package butter chocolate cake mix
3 eggs
1 21-ounce can cherry pie filling
1 cup sugar
5 tablespoons butter
1/3 cup milk
1 6-ounce package semi-sweet chocolate chips

Mix first three ingredients until well blended. Pour into a greased and floured 9 x 12 inch pan and bake at 350 degrees for 35 to 40 minutes. For icing, combine sugar, butter, and milk. Bring to a boil, stirring constantly; boil for 1 minute. Remove from heat and stir in chocolate chips, blending until smooth. Spread on cake.

Lola Carson's Jam Cake

1/2 pound butter
3 cups brown sugar
4 egg yolks, beaten
1 teaspoon baking soda
1 cup buttermilk
4 cups flour
1 cup blackberry jam
1 cup strawberry preserves
1 cup pecans
1 cup raisins
1 teaspoon cinnamon
1 teaspoon cloves
1 teaspoon allspice
1 teaspoon nutmeg
6 tablespoons port wine
6 tablespoons "4 Roses" whiskey
4 egg whites, beaten

Cream butter and sugar. Add well-beaten egg yolks. Beat soda into buttermilk with a spoon. Add alternately with flour (use one cup flour with nuts and raisins). Add remainder of ingredients except egg whites. Mix well. Fold in beaten egg whites. Use stem pan, greased and floured with brown paper on bottom. Bake at 300 degrees for 2 hours and 30 minutes.

Note: Exactly as given to Sis Michael in 1944!

Snow Ball Cake

2 packages unflavored gelatin
4 teaspoons cold water
1 cup boiling water
1 cup crushed pineapple, undrained
1 cup sugar
1/2 teaspoon salt
1/2 teaspoon lemon juice
3 envelopes Dream Whip
(prepared as directed on package)
1 angel food cake
coconut

Dissolve gelatin in cold water; add boiling water and set aside to cool. Combine pineapple, sugar, salt, and lemon juice; add to gelatin mixture. Let this congeal slightly and fold in two boxes of prepared Dream Whip. Remove brown crust from angel food cake and break into bite size pieces. Line bowl with wax paper or foil. Alternate layers of gelatin mixture with layers of cake pieces. End with a layer of congealed gelatin mixture. Let stand over night in refrigerator.

Turn out onto cake plate. Top with remaining box of prepared Dream Whip and cover with coconut. Store in refrigerator.

Amaretto Cake

1 package plain yellow cake mix,
1 small package lemon instant pudding
2 tablespoons Amaretto
1/2 cup + 2 tablespoons water
1/2 cup oil
4 eggs

In mixing bowl, combine cake mix, pudding mix, Amaretto, water and oil. Add eggs, one at a time, beating well after each addition. Pour into greased and floured tube pan. Bake at 325 degrees for 45 minutes to 1 hour or until cake tests done. After cake has cooled, spoon glaze over top.

Glaze:
2 cups powdered sugar
2 tablespoons orange juice
2 tablespoons Amaretto
1 teaspoon orange rind, grated

Mix all ingredients together.

Lemon Pound Cake

4 eggs
1 package plain yellow cake mix
1 small package lemon instant pudding
3/4 cup water
1/3 cup salad oil

Combine all ingredients. Bake at 350 degrees until done. Remove from pan and top with Lemon Glaze, below.

Lemon Glaze:
2 cups powdered sugar
1/3 cup lemon juice

Heat sugar and lemon juice to boiling. Spoon on top of cooled cake.

On a Saturday night following Christmas we did a wedding reception for a very special bride. I went overboard on the size of the cake. Very, very tall. I assembled it on the table early and it was a masterpiece. Someone came in and said "I went out to look at the cake and it wasn't on the table." I thought, oh they looked at the wrong table. But, no! It had fallen to the floor. Norma, being hostess on a very busy Saturday night, came to the rescue. It was forty-five minutes before time for guests to come into the room. A miracle was performed by my "miracle worker". The cake was even lovelier the second time around!

Mama's Eggplant Pudding Cake

1 package plain yellow cake mix
1 small package vanilla instant pudding
4 eggs
1 cup sour cream
1/4 cup oil
2 cups eggplant, peeled and grated
1/2 teaspoon nutmeg
1/4 teaspoon cinnamon
1/4 teaspoon cloves
1/4 teaspoon salt
powdered sugar, optional

Combine all ingredients except powdered sugar. Beat at medium speed with electric mixer for 4 minutes. Pour into greased and floured tube pan and bake at 350 degrees for 70 minutes or until cake tests done. Do not underbake. Cool in pan for 15 minutes. Remove from pan and place on rack to finish cooling. Sprinkle sifted powdered sugar on top, if desired. For mellowing of flavors, cover and store overnight.

Chocolate Chip Cake from Hannah Till

1 box yellow cake mix
1 small box instant vanilla pudding
1 small box instant chocolate pudding
4 eggs
1 1/2 cups water
1/2 cup oil
1 6-ounce package chocolate chips

Empty cake mix and puddings into bowl. Stir until mixed, then add eggs, water and oil. Blend well, then beat for 2 minutes at medium speed. Add chocolate chips and stir in with a spoon. Bake in a greased and floured bundt pan at 350 degrees for 1 hour. Cool for 20 minutes and remove from pan.

This cake may be iced with your favorite chocolate icing, or you could sprinkle top with powdered sugar.

Tomato Soup Spice Cake

1 package spice cake mix
1 can condensed tomato soup
1/4 cup water
1/2 cup raisins
1/2 cup pecans, chopped

Prepare cake mix according to package directions using tomato soup and 1/4 cup water as liquid. Stir in raisins and pecans. Bake in two greased and lightly floured 8 x 1 1/2-inch round cake pans. Bake at 325 degrees for 30 to 35 minutes or until done. Cool in pans 10 minutes. Remove from pans and when completely cooled frost with the following:

Golden Butter Frosting:
1/2 cup butter, softened
1 egg yolk
2 tablespoons buttermilk
1/2 teaspoon vanilla
3 cups powdered sugar, sifted

Beat together softened butter, egg yolk, buttermilk and vanilla. Gradually adding powdered sugar until well mixed.

Serves 12

Aunt Ruth's Dried Apple Cake

2 1/2 cups dried apples, cooked
1 cup butter, room temperature
2 cups sugar
4 cups flour
4 teaspoons soda
4 teaspoons cinnamon
4 teaspoons nutmeg
1 box raisins, dusted with flour
1 cup dates, chopped
1 cup pecans, chopped

Mix apples, while still hot, with butter and sugar. Add remaining ingredients. Bake at 300 degrees for 1 1/2 hours in a greased and floured tube pan. Remove from oven, let cool for 10 minutes. Remove from pan and cool completely. Wrap with cloth soaked in wine. Store in airtight container.

A wonderfully heavy moist cake.

Zona's "Memaw's" Sherbet

1 carton half and half
1 medium can crushed pineapple
strawberries as desired, fresh or frozen
1 cup orange juice
1/2 cup lemon juice
3 cups sugar
3 bananas, mashed
whole milk

Mix all together, stirring to dissolve sugar. Pour into a 4-quart ice cream freezer and finish filling with whole milk. Freeze until firm.

Lou Ester's Buttermilk Sherbet

2 cups buttermilk
1 cup sugar
1 8-ounce can crushed pineapple
1 tablespoon vanilla
2 egg whites, room temperature

Combine buttermilk, sugar, undrained pineapple and vanilla. Mix well. Place in an airtight container; freeze until slushy.

Beat egg whites until stiff peaks form. Add buttermilk mixture and beat well. Pour into airtight freezer container and return to freezer; freeze until firm.

Yields 1 quart

Kathy's Ice Cream

4 eggs, beaten
2 1/2 cups sugar
2 1/2 tablespoons vanilla
1/2 teaspoon salt
3 cups whipping cream
7 cups milk

Mix all ingredients. Pour into a one gallon ice cream freezer; freeze according to manufacturer's directions.

For Brandy Alexander Ice Cream:
Omit 1 1/2 cups milk and add 1 cup brandy and 1/2 cup crème de cocoa.

Caramel Layer Brownies

1 14 to 16-ounce bag wrapped caramel candy chews (50 chews)
1/3 cup evaporated milk or half and half
1 package German Chocolate cake mix
2/3 cup butter, melted
1/3 cup evaporated milk or half and half, for cake
1 cup walnuts or pecans, chopped
12 ounces chocolate chips

Melt together caramels and 1/3 cup evaporated milk or half and half in top of double boiler; set aside.

Combine cake mix, butter, milk and nuts. Lightly pat half of mixture in 9 x 13 inch pan coated with cooking spray. Bake at 350 degrees for 6 minutes. Remove from oven and sprinkle chocolate chips evenly over cake. Pour melted caramel over this. Crumble other half of cake mix evenly over all. Bake 16 to 18 minutes. Cool and refrigerate a few hours before serving. Cut into bars.

Bunny's Devastating Chocolate Fudge Pie

1/2 cup butter
3 1-ounce squares unsweetened chocolate
4 eggs, beaten
3 tablespoons light corn syrup
1 1/2 cups sugar
1/4 teaspoon salt
1 teaspoon vanilla
1 9-inch pastry shell, unbaked

In top of double boiler, over boiling water, heat butter and chocolate, stirring until melted and well-blended; allow to cool slightly. Blend syrup, sugar, salt and vanilla into beaten eggs. Add chocolate mixture; blend well. Pour mixture into pie shell. Bake at 325 degrees for 45 minutes or until pie is almost but not quite firm when shaken.

Serves 6 to 8

Chocolate Mint Supremes

1 cup sugar
1 stick margarine, softened
1 16-ounce can chocolate syrup
1 cup flour
4 eggs, beaten
1 6-ounce package chocolate chips
1 stick margarine
1 3-ounce package cream cheese
1/2 stick margarine, softened
4 cups powdered sugar
4 tablespoons milk
3 teaspoons peppermint extract
green food coloring

Blend sugar, margarine, chocolate syrup, flour and eggs. Pour mixture into a greased 9 x 13 inch pan. Bake at 350 degrees for 25 minutes. Cool. Beat cheese, softened margarine, powdered sugar, milk and peppermint extract until smooth and creamy. Add a few drops of green coloring. Spread over cooled chocolate cake. Refrigerate 45 minutes. Melt chocolate chips with 1 stick margarine and spread over cooled mint layer. Chill, then cut into small squares.

Pecan Crispies

1 cup butter or margarine
1/2 cup sugar
1 teaspoon vanilla
1/2 cup crushed potato chips
1/2 cup chopped pecans
2 cups sifted flour

Cream butter, sugar and vanilla. Add crushed potato chips and pecans. Stir in flour. Roll into small balls. Place on ungreased cookie sheet and press ball flat with bottom of tumbler dipped in sugar. Bake at 350 degrees for 16 to 18 minutes or until lightly browned.

Makes approximately 3 dozen cookies

Dream Bars

1 cup flour
1/2 cup sugar
1/2 cup butter

Mix flour, sugar and butter; press in pan and cook at 350 degrees for 10 minutes while preparing the filling.

Filling:
3 eggs
1 cup brown sugar
1 cup coconut
1/2 cup pecans
1 teaspoon vanilla

Beat eggs, add sugar gradually, then remaining ingredients. Pour over flour, sugar and butter mixture. Bake for 15 minutes more or until done.

Chocolate Chip Meringues

2 egg whites
dash salt
1/4 teaspoon cream of tartar
3/4 cup sugar
1 6-ounce package chocolate chips
peppermint to taste

Beat egg whites with salt and cream of tartar until frothy. Gradually add sugar and continue to beat for 15 minutes. Fold in chocolate chips and peppermint. Drop by teaspoonfuls on an ungreased cookie sheet. Place in a preheated 350 degree oven and turn off oven. Leave in oven for 1 1/2 hours. Do not open oven door to peek.

Makes 36 candies

Janice Grace's Schaum Torte

6 egg whites
2 cups sugar
1 teaspoon vanilla
1 teaspoon vinegar
strawberries
whipped cream

Whip egg whites until stiff. Add sugar gradually; then add vanilla and vinegar. Pour into greased springform pan and bake at 300 degrees for 1 hour.

Serve topped with strawberries and whipped cream.

Miscellaneous Recipes

Snowy White Frosting

4 egg whites
2 tablespoons water
1/4 teaspoon cream of tartar
1/2 teaspoon salt
4 1/2 cups powdered sugar
2 teaspoons vanilla
marachino cherries

Combine egg whites, water, cream of tartar and salt in large bowl. Beat at high speed of electric mixer until egg whites are stiff but not dry. Gradually add powdered sugar and beat until stiff peaks form. Fold in vanilla. Frost cake layers. Top with maraschino cherries.

Chocolate Icing

2 sticks margarine
8 tablespoons cocoa
12 tablespoons milk
2 pounds powdered sugar, sifted

Bring margarine, cocoa and milk to a boil. Add to powdered sugar which has been placed in a large bowl. Cool slightly, then beat lightly. Don't beat too much as this gets hard quickly.

Caramel Icing

1/2 cup butter
1 cup firmly packed brown sugar
1/4 cup cream
1 1/2 cups sifted powdered sugar

Melt butter over low heat. Blend brown sugar and cream, stirring constantly. Bring to boil for one minute. Remove from heat, cool until lukewarm. When cool add powdered sugar and beat.

Orange Filling for Meringues

3 egg yolks
2 tablespoons sugar
salt
6 tablespoons frozen orange juice concentrate
1 1/2 teaspoons orange rind, grated
1 cup heavy cream, whipped
18 orange sections, sweetened

Beat egg yolks in top of double boiler. Add sugar, salt and orange juice concentrate. Cook over boiling water, stirring constantly, until thickened. Remove from heat; add orange rind and chill. Fold in whipped cream. Spoon into meringues just before serving. Spoon orange sections over meringues.

Rhubarb Jam

5 cups rhubarb, cut into 3/4 inch lengths
4 cups sugar
1 small box strawberry gelatin

Boil rhubarb and sugar for 10 minutes. (Use no water as sugar and rhubarb will form liquid.) Add gelatin and stir. Pour in glass jars and seal, or pour into plastic containers and freeze.

Zucchini Marmalade

6 cups peeled and shredded zucchini
1/2 cup lemon juice
1 cup crushed pineapple, drained
1 package Sure Jell
6 cups sugar
6 ounces apricot gelatin, or your favorite flavor

Cook zucchini for one hour on low heat. Add lemon juice, pineapple and Sure Jell and stir well. Add sugar and cook 6 minutes, then stir in gelatin while hot.

Pour into 4 one-pint jars which have been sterilized, then seal.

Makes 4 pints

Fire Logs

old newspapers
3 gallons water
3 pounds rock salt
1 pound blue stone
old containers

> Caution: Protect hands and arms while preparing and using liquid mixture and be careful of fumes from mixture. This should be prepared outside or with plenty of ventilation.

Roll papers into logs the size you like. Tie tightly with sturdy string. Heat water, rock salt and stone in old container. Mix together until melted. Place paper logs standing up in another old container and slowly pour liquid mixture over logs. Let stand until dry.

Shirley Jean's Special Bird Food

1 cup peanut butter
1 cup shortening
1 cup all-purpose flour
4 cups plain cornmeal

Cream peanut butter and shortening. Add flour and cornmeal. Birds will almost eat from your hand.

Spiced Salt

3/4 cups salt
2 tablespoons sugar
2 tablespoons paprika
2 teaspoons ground black pepper
2 teaspoons onion powder
2 teaspoons hot dry mustard
2 teaspoons ground allspice
1 teaspoon garlic powder
2 teaspoons ground coriander

Mix all ingredients well and store in tightly covered containers or salt or seasoning shakers.

Use as an all-purpose seasoned salt for eggs, potatoes, or salads.

Makes 1 1/4 cups

To Freeze Stock

Freeze meat or chicken stock in ice cube trays. Put in plastic bags and keep in freezer to season sauces and soups. Remove frozen cubes as needed.

Index

COOK TALK WITH CURTIS GRACE AND FRIENDS

Mail to:
McClanahan Publishing House, Inc.
P.O. Box 100
Kuttawa, Kentucky 42055

For Orders CALL TOLL FREE
1-800-544-6959
Visa & MasterCard accepted

Please send me___________copies of

COOKTALK WITH CURTIS GRACE AND FRIENDS	**@ $14.00 each**	_____
Postage and Handling	**@ $2.00 each**	_____
Kentucky residents add 5% sales tax	**@ .70 each**	_____
Total		_____

Make check payable to McClanahan Publishing House

Ship to:
Name____

Address______________________________________

City____________________State________Zip__________

- -

COOK TALK WITH CURTIS GRACE AND FRIENDS

Mail to:
McClanahan Publishing House, Inc.
P.O. Box 100
Kuttawa, Kentucky 42055

For Orders CALL TOLL FREE
1-800-544-6959
Visa & MasterCard accepted

Please send me___________copies of

COOKTALK WITH CURTIS GRACE AND FRIENDS	**@ $14.00 each**	_____
Postage and Handling	**@ $2.00 each**	_____
Kentucky residents add 5% sales tax	**@ .70 each**	_____
Total		_____

Make check payable to McClanahan Publishing House

Ship to:
Name____

Address______________________________________

City____________________State________Zip__________